Published by:
LIVING TIME ® Digital
Kemp House, 152-160 City Road
London EC1V 2NX
United Kingdom.

ISBN 978-1-903331-59-0

British Library *Cataloguing in Publication* Data.
A Bibliographic (*CIP*) Catalogue record is
available from The British Library.

email: info@livingtime.co.uk
website: www.livingtime.net
telephone: 02071014141
rights: 07930-128892

THE EXPERIENCE
OF DEATH

and The Moral Problem of Suicide

*"The human race is the only one
that knows it must die, and it knows
this only through its experience"*

VOLTAIRE

Paul Louis
Landsberg

LIVING TIME® Press

Editor's Note

This volume has been one of the most 'popular' volumes that *Living Time* ® has issued since it first started publishing in 1999. Surprising, in one sense, because it deals with topics that are, to many people, both unattractive and to be avoided if possible. Death is hardly 'coffee-table talk', and suicide is a subject that is generally ignored rather than being thought about or discussed. Probably the greatest benefit of the two works contained in this book is that neither of them has any desire to force the reader to firm and definite conclusions, but what each of them achieves is to take the reader on a journey through the area of discussion which allows whoever is reading to confront the reality and the issues themselves. Perhaps it is the case that we are attracted by what we fear, and no matter what our feelings are about death and suicide, we are drawn to want to know more, we are curious to find out what they are. Whether this book by Landsberg can teach you this, I, as editor, am not able to say. That is what you will find out in the course of perusing this volume. - The bulk of this publication has been unaltered since the previous edition, however, the changes meriting a mention are that there is a short note and bibliography of the author (that were absent before), as well as an image of Landsberg and a revised front cover. For an alternative treatment of the philosophy of death readers are recommended to turn to 'Being and Time' by Martin Heidegger, where an analysis is made of the same subject. He is also an existentlaist.

EDOUARD d'ARAILLE, SERIES EDITOR - JULY 2008, LTP™.

PAGEFINDER

Editor's Note i

Note on the Author iv

Acknowledgements v

The Experience of Death 1

I The State of the Question 3

II The Limitations of Scheler's Answer 6

III Individualism and the Experience of Death 9

IV The Death of a Friend,
and the Experience of "Repetition" 13

V The Ontological Basis 23

VI The Death of a Friend, according to the Fourth
Book of the Confessions of St. Augustine 29

VII The Forms of Experience of Death 34

VIII Intermezzo in the Bull Ring 45

IX The Christian Experience of Death 50

The Moral Problem of Suicide

1. Traditional Arguments 67

2. A Personal View 89

Annotations 101

Note on the Author

Paul Louis Landsberg was born in Bonn in 1901. Having completed his studies he went on to become Professor of Philosophy at the university of this city, however, due to his opposition to nazism he fled Germany one day before the coming to power of Hitler in 1933. Between 1934 and 1936 he held lecturing positions in Madrid and Barcelona, where his thought exerted a great influence over his pupils and where it is still studied avidly to this day. However, with the coming of the Civil War in Spain Landsberg transferred to Paris where he gave courses at the Sorbonne on the meaning of existence, at which time he also became closely involved with the journal 'Esprit', where his thought was very influential. At this time he also became friends with the 'Personalist' philosopher Emmanuel Mounier, whose themes were similar to those studied in his own works. A friend of Max Scheler's, and a disciple of some of his phenomenological methods, Landsberg was like him a Christian. He was hounded by the Gestapo for a long period of time and In 1943 Landsberg was deported from Paris for being of Jewish origin. He was transported to the Work Camp at Oranienburg, Berlin, where he died of exhaustion in 1944.

SELECT BIBLIOGRAPHY

The Essence and Meaning of the Platonic Academy (1923)

The Vocation of Pascal (1927)

Introduction to Philosophical Anthropology (1934)

The Conception of the Person (Essay in *Esprit*, 1934)

The Experience of Death (1937)

The Moral Problem of Suicide (1937)

The Philosophy of St. Augustine (1944)

Machiavelli, a Study (1944)

Acknowledgements

Living Time ® **Press** takes this opportunity to acknowledge its debt of gratitude to all those who have invested their time and effort in the production of this revised edition of the Kerr translation of Landsberg's seminal studies of Death and Suicide. Her translation is very accurate in its rendition of the texts, and it has been reproduced insofar as the language has not been outdated. However, in numerous instances the orthography and the vocabulary have been judged to be obsolete and in need of revision so as to be readily understandable by the contemporary reader. Throughout the process of revision the editor has made reference to the original, ensuring that its content and meaning are not lost at any point. Furthermore, reference has been made to the other translations of the work (for example, the Spanish) so as to consider the language decisions that have been made by different translators. The translations presented here are based on the texts from 1937, the only difference in detail being that we have chosen to place the annotations at the close of the volume, seeing that some of these are lengthy and may distract from the overall flow of the discussion. Brief biographical details are given on the front inside cover, including a select bibliography of works by Landsberg.

ALDERSON SMITH, LONDON, AUGUST 2002

v

THE EXPERIENCE OF DEATH

"It is entirely impossible for a thinking being to think of its own non-existence, of the termination of its thinking and life"

J.W. von GOETHE

Paul Louis

Landsberg

PARIS, 1937

The Experience of Death

WHAT is the meaning of death to the human being as a person? The question admits of no conclusion, for we are dealing with the very mystery of man, taken from a certain aspect. Every real problem in philosophy contains all the others in the unity of mystery.

It is necessary, therefore, to set a limit and seek a basis in experience for any possible answer : there are always problems of the utmost importance left on one side. Our enquiry would seem inevitable in the present state of philosophy, for we are far from having a metaphysics of death, as we have of life.

PAUL LOUIS LANDSBERG

2

I The State of the Question

"THE human race is the only one that knows it must die, and it knows this only through its experience," Voltaire, his mind often more unquiet than we suppose, thus sets the problem in its true light at the very beginning of his treatise on man.[1]

Let us consider more closely the two theses contained in this highly significant statement. Each assertion is open to a dual interpretation, an interpretation which can, on the one hand, lead us into error, and on the other, open to us the heart of the matter. If man is the sole living being to know that he must die, we should remember that certain animals have, as it were, a presentiment of death, yet, to tell the truth, solely when they are threatened by its immediate presence. Then they lay themselves down and wait for death, with a calmness and dignity of manner that misanthropists have preferred to that of many humans.

But this sort of presentiment, this perception of the immediate, is not, properly speaking, knowledge, and even if it could be transformed into the corresponding knowledge, it would still fail to be a knowledge of the necessity of death. The animal would not, for instance, be aware that the death of the individual is essential to life and to the species. The comprehension of the link between birth and death, the biological necessity that the individual should disappear to the benefit of the species, and that the

3

species should disappear in favour of the realisation of the ever-changing forms of life — such comprehension is no doubt solely reserved to man. The origin of such speculations can be found, for instance, in the inverse proportion between the power of propagation and the specific duration of existence in the species, or in the causal and temporal link between propagation and death so obvious in the life history of many creatures. It goes equally without saying that such speculations occur relatively late in the history of the human mind. Yet even such reflections are not the original source of the human certainty with regard to death. Voltaire points out that here we are dealing with an experience of which the real content is not the fact of dying, but the certainty that we have to die.

Voltaire's thesis lends itself easily to the empirical interpretation of his age. There are at hand countless instances of cases of individual deaths, on the strength of which the empiricism of the encyclopedists would have us admit the necessity of dying, on the same grounds that we admit the necessity of the sun's rising in the East.

This would, of course, only constitute an approximate necessity, and a conclusion drawn from the correspondence of a great number of cases would not stand up to the scepticism of a Hume. Neither would man ever despair of overcoming this necessity. The specifically human element would be reduced to the rational capacity to embrace the sum of a great number of individual cases, and of abstracting, by induction, a law of reality. This element would then depend, not on the mode and content of the experience itself, but on the way in which man can utilise it to arrive at general laws and rational truths. And Voltaire's saying would become part and parcel of the dominant anthropology of his epoch, which was able to define man as a rational being.[2]

It would seem, however, that these words "its experience" have an objective content greater than Voltaire clearly perceived himself, and it is this obscurer, more effective content which leads us towards a fresh enquiry.

Is there a specific experience of death, through which one might learn that death was natural to man in the wholeness of his personal life? And this experience, which already allows us to establish the fact of considerable probability, does it not also confront us with the fact of necessity?

I I The Limitations of Scheler's Answer

PHENOMENOLOGY has taught us that human experience is qualitatively richer than is admitted by the concept of experience as provided by classical empiricism. It has also shown that the content of experience is not the mere co-existence of isolated data, but also essential structures and relationships. It is along these lines that Scheler has tried to restate the theory of biological experience and to discover the true nature of the human experience of death.[3] But we cannot be satisfied with his reply to our question. What he has described, in his profound and deeply illuminating manner, is the experience of growing old. According to him, the idea of death occurs only as a limiting point, which one may foresee by observing the development of the process of growing old. The structure of our life changes noticeably at every moment. The pressure of the past grows heavier, and the possibilities of the future more narrow. Man feels himself less and less free, less and less capable of transforming the meaning of his life by shaping his future. As he grows old, he loses not only the sense of freedom but, to a certain degree, freedom itself. Here, no doubt, is a terrible truth. But is not death, to human experience, something other than the concept of the final limit of individual evolution? Here, for the first time, we meet the problems raised by our capacity to have a dual experience of death. We may be aware of it, on the one hand as the immanent future of our own life, or as the death of the *other*, that we witness, or of which we are indirectly aware. It is mainly through this second form that we know that death is in no sense linked with the process of growing old. In most cases it intervenes quite early, biologically speaking, and it can only be considered "natural" in very rare cases where it does, in fact, appear as the culmination of old age. But even in these rare cases, there must still arise the little, exceptional accident : a cold, an inflammation, a diarrhoea, to which the organism is no longer resistant. The specific character of so-called natural death can be recognised by the absence of any obvious struggle between the forces of resistance and the forces of dissolution. The resistance of life has simply become too weak. On the other hand, a violent illness is only the struggle which indicates the organism's power of resistance. But man's experience of the necessity of his own death has nothing in common with the hypothesis of the natural death of the organism. It is evident to me, not only that I must die once, that is to say, when I have reached the limiting point of natural death, but also that I am face to face, at every moment of my life, now and always, with the immediate possibility of death. Death is very close to me. Human uncertainty with regard to death is not merely the result of a lacuna in biology, but also of my ignorance of my destiny, and even this "ignorance" is an act in which there is a presence as well as an absence of death. *Mors certa, hora incerta.* The dialectic of death is secret. It is an absent presence. Thus the problem of the human experience of the necessity of death reaches beyond biology, just as it reaches beyond the data provided by the feeling of growing old.

III Individualism and the Experience of Death

BUT is man capable of an experience of such a kind? It can be said that, under certain conditions, he may be. It is probably by becoming aware of these conditions that we can best approach the specific element of such experience.

The two most important categories of human beings who seem unaware of the necessity of death, are children and primitive peoples. We have learnt, from the investigations of Lévy-Bruhl, the nature of the concept of death which governs the mentality of primitive peoples. Since to them death has always an external cause, it is therefore fortuitous. In primitive societies the individual is not sufficiently differentiated from his clan to be able to individualise himself in any other way than by his position in the clan and by his function in the social organism. If, on his death, another individual succeeds to this position, the latter also acquires the name and soul of the dead man. The clan has regenerated its lost member. And it is as if nothing had happened. As in the animal species the law of regeneration conceals the effect of individual death. Men, according to the classic simile, are like the leaves on the tree. Death is only the passage of the soul into a new individual, the other side of birth.

We may therefore observe a historical phenomenon which is so general that it may be adduced as a law:

an awareness of death goes hand in hand with human individualisation, the constitution of the person. This individualisation is not primarily the acquisition of a clearer, more defined awareness of personal singularity : it is first of all the fact that man does really gain in singularity. A change of awareness presupposes a change of being. Thus it is not primarily the awareness of an individual death which grows more intense, but rather the sense of the menace of such death. The individual endows it with a content proper to him alone, which must therefore exceed the limits of the clan, regeneration by the clan and rebirth within the clan. It is only from this moment that he conceives a factor capable of being threatened by real annihilation; that is to say, that he conceives the possibility of individual death. The effect of this evolution explains why periods of history which are rich in examples of individualisation are periods haunted by the thought of death. The mysteries and the philosophies of late antiquity, which are more closely connected than is generally supposed, are almost exclusively determined by this individual anguish. The negative phenomenon is then the dissolution of the antique city ; the positive phenomenon, a new degree of human individuality ; its consequence, a new anguish in the concept of death ; and its final product, the mysteries, the philosophic sects, the preparation of Christianity. In the same way the mediæval community dissolves in the period of the Renaissance and the Reformation; once more we perceive a highly individualised humanity, in torment at the increasing menace of death. It is a period of panic anguish, a period in theology dominated by the need of the individual to know justification at the moment of death, a period picturing the Dance of Death, giving a cruelly realistic portrayal of Christ dead on the Cross or in the Tomb.[4]

The content of the new doctrine of survival which became possible and necessary with this new sense of death is entirely different from the former confidence in regeneration through the clan. The fact of survival is no paradox to the primitive mind : it is not even particularly agreeable. With them the fear of the dead is far greater than their fear of death.[5] They fear the still unreincarnated dead as beings who are close at hand, hidden and menacing. They see them as possible ghosts who must be satisfied and charmed away by ritual mainly designed to prevent them from doing harm. The higher religions which promise victory over death are not addressed to peoples who believe that after death there is only the expectation of nothingness, but they assume certain beliefs in survival of a different character. In India, before the coming of Buddha, the sense of being imprisoned in the eternal cycle of death and rebirth had become intolerable to the conscious individual. The deliverance promised by Buddha, can be at one and the same time deliverance from birth and death and from the birth and re-birth which are the condition of death. The Christian concept of survival, understood in its relationship to the ontological category of eternity represents a final liberation from the time and change and earthly becoming which imply death. The individual finds himself, as it were, lifted above the stream of generations. But Christ promises a birth which shall be followed by no death. Buddha promises a death which shall be followed by no birth and thus by no further death. Christianity is the supreme affirmation of victorious life.[6] Buddhism is the negation of life by very virtue of the reality of death. Buddhism presupposes the Brahmin belief according to which the sequence of birth and death is all the more indestructible in that it is inherent in the very essence of reality. Christianity presupposes the Jewish faith according to which this sequence is solely due to original sin and can therefore be broken in virtue of a new birth, by the intervention of divine Grace, which will triumph over sin and, by the same act, over death.

I U The Death of a Friend, and the Experience of "Repetition"

WE must admit then that a decisive experience of death is bound up with a certain degree of awareness of personal uniqueness, and that the process of individualisation and of becoming conscious of death go hand in hand. In order to grasp this thesis entirely, we start from the experience of the death of the other, which has obviously a peculiar quality for those who are still living.

We need not claim that this is the only possible point of departure. There are states very similar to death which, up to a certain point, are still part of the experience we can have of ourselves ; deep sleep, certain types of unconsciousness, the vague recollection of an embryonic pre-natal state which can be recalled by a form of meditation, and so on. There is also an experience of death in undergoing the danger of death, as in war, serious illness or accidents. There are a thousand ways of foreseeing and envisaging one's own death. Some saints have known the hour of their death by meditation, some doctors by science, some heroes by decision. But in each of these experiences, the essential difference between dying and death, between undergoing as an act and that which one undergoes, is necessarily hidden. We cannot, by following these experiences, transcend the physiology of dying in a metaphysics of death itself. If we take our point of departure from the expe-

13

rience of the death of the other, we may hope in this way to meet the *person* as such and the specific relationship it may have to death.[7]

In so far as we individualise ourselves, we observe the uniqueness of others. In personal love we grasp this uniqueness in its untellable quality and in its essential difference from ourselves. The death of a man we love with such a love should tell us something decisive which reaches beyond the domain of biological fact. The death of one's neighbour is infinitely more than just the death of another. Where there is a question of the *person* we may reach the possibility of an ontological relationship to death. The only means of extracting from authentic experience all the meaning it contains is to re-live it in memory.

First of all we perceive a process being completed in the organism of the other. Here he is presented to us as essentially a living body. It is, perhaps, the crisis of the illness through which death will intervene. We know that the person we love still exists as such, only he is hidden behind this process, though he may perhaps reappear at times, for instance, in a few last brief words. But the dominant fact is this, that a living body is suffering : our own body suffers in the flesh with that of our suffering comrade.[8] And then there comes a moment when all is calm, when all seems to be over and the contorted features of the well-loved face relax. It is precisely at this moment, when the living being abandons us, that we shall experience the mysterious absence of the person as spirit. For a moment we have a feeling of relief. The suffering of our bodily sympathy is over — but immediately we

14

are carried away into the strange cold world of death fulfilled. The vital pity we felt is thus suspended in a void and suddenly gives way to the profound awareness that this being, in all the uniqueness of his person, is no longer there, and can no more return into this body. He will never speak to us again, he will never live again in community with us as he used to do. Never again.

The higher forms of faith in survival are in complete agreement with this experience. They speak of the spiritual personality not as annihilated, but only as if vanished, as if existing in absence. If death were the absent presence, then the dead man is now present absence.[9] The immediate experience of the death of the other does not at first offer us any certainty of his survival. It presents us with the fact of absence and says nothing as to whether this is a sequel to annihilation or only a disappearance with regard to ourselves. The belief in survival promises us that our own death will reunite us with him who has disappeared, that we shall once more hear his voice in unknown circumstances, and liberated from the former body. But a pure and simple experience of death does nothing either to confirm or to destroy this promise. In any case, it is a purely human experience, for it assumes there has been some realisation of two kindred principles which are essentially human : a spiritual personalisation and a personal love for one's friend. We see, too, that since death intervenes as the "unknown" it must exceed all experience of illness, suffering or old age.

The experience of the death of a friend is unique each time that it occurs. Here we meet death in its own personal uniqueness. Each death is as unique as each person's manner of being present. But an intuition of the necessity of death may then arise. The eyes of the spirit have been able to grasp the intimate connection between an event of vital importance and the disappearance of the *person*. The person becomes absent after this strange fashion at the very moment when the vital process in a given organism reaches its end. This change of relationship may be recognised as characteristic and necessary to all experiences of such a kind. The living body becomes a corpse. But a corpse is no longer a possible place for the person to inhabit.[10] Even the aspect of the corpse teaches us not only that the vital process proper to a human being is here drawn to an end, but also, the moment we introduce the category of the person, that a personal spirit can no longer dwell in this body. In the open eyes of the corpse we perceive not only the end of life but also the disappearance of the person as spirit. We see that the one can no longer be present because the other is no longer there. Life in the biological sense shows by its end that it is the basis of presence, an indispensable basis for the realisation of the spiritual personality in the human being.

But all this is still not an experience of the necessity of death; it only makes us aware in a special way of the truly multiple structure of our terrestrial existence. The awareness of the necessity of death is only provoked by participation, by the personal love

in which the whole experience is bathed. We consti-
tuted a "we" with the dying man, And it is through this
"we", through the very strength of this community,
which constitutes, as it were, a new order of persons,
that we are led into an experiential knowledge of our
own mortality. For a moment we have our feet in the
land of the dead. A moment later we are once more
outside the kingdom of shadows. But during that
moment we experienced its bitter cold. And no one
is ever quite the same after he has felt it.

The sense of the necessity of death, which is our
focus here, is not identical with the sense of a general statement of necessity, which allots any one form
of death to any one of our species. The necessity is
chiefly related to those whom we love and to ourselves. This sphere, within which we are really aware
of the threat of death, is surrounded by a vague,
obscure horizon, filled with other human figures,
real and possible, past and future. The concepts of
necessity and generality are never as closely allied
as rationalism would have us suppose. We are often
able to conceive a relationship of necessity which in
fact only exists with regard to one individual personality and which is derived precisely from that individuality. The experience of death does in fact provide a
synthesis of necessity and generality. But both are of
a very special kind. The general necessity here is not
of a logical but rather of a symbolic nature. The *other*
represents in reality all the others. He is Everyman,
and this Everyman dies each time in the death of the
man we know, who dies his own death.[11] A reality is
symbolised here which is unique and universal in

17

exactly the same way as is the necessity of death.[12] As a biologist, I may note the finite character of possible existence inherent in any given organism, that is to say, the fact that living implies a constant struggle against obstacles and dangers and that every organism must in the long run exhaust its energies in this struggle. But this is still a rationalisation of Scheler's intuition of death as a limiting point. But what is added by a lived experience is the coincidence between this limiting point in biology and the sudden disappearance of spirituality. Hence the generality and necessity of the connection. There is an existential problem which becomes clear in the painful knowledge that there is no possibility of any further exteriorised communication between us and the dead man, not at any rate through his voice which we knew so well. Those lips will no longer speak to me. Those glazed eyes will no longer see me. My community with this person seems shattered, but the community was to some degree myself, and to this degree I experience death in the very core of my own existence. It is the experience of death in the solitude that follows loss. There is in this decisive experience of the death of a friend something like a sense of tragic infidelity in his departure, just as there is an experience of death in our reaction to infidelity. "I am dead to him, he is dead to me", is not a figure of speech, it is the abyss. Theologians and mystics tell us that only God is faithful, for God alone does not die, that death itself is the outcome of a wilful infidelity which plunges the whole world into that ontological infidelity which is our mortality. All these revealed truths correspond to the experience described, although of course they cannot be deduced from it.

Many observers have remarked that the experience of death had only a negligible effect on the soldiers of the First World War, that is to say, whilst the fighting was going on. An army doctor has said that in this sense, death was a civilian idea.[13] One reason is that the personal experience of the death of a comrade does not occur simultaneously with his death, but succeeds it in time. If our duty summons us immediately to new activity, the moment of the presence of death itself must necessarily be lost. It seems, however, undeniable that this personal experience is only postponed to a time when its essential pre-requisite, a personal community with the dead man, can be realised. For this it is not even necessary that there should have been a personal friendship. A single act of personal love is enough to reveal to me, by creating the presence, or rather the present absence of the person, the essence of human death. A single moment of calm in the presence of the dead, even if he be an unknown enemy — and the situation may provoke an act of personal love towards one's neighbour as such. Then the concept of human mortality recovers its full dignity.

The concrete example we took as our point of departure served no more than to awaken intuition. We imagined ourselves, largely through the help of memory, watching the outcome of a fatal illness. The eyes of the mind saw the final struggle between life and death drawing to its close ; they saw it succeeded by the spiritual mystery of death fulfilled. But it is not necessary to be in fact, or by repeated effort of the imagination, present at this final struggle in order to distinguish in perfect clarity the essence of the experience. The suffering of relatives of soldiers killed in the war, involved a similar experience. They felt it when they received the fatal letter confronting them, as with the accomplished fact, with the spiritual presence of the death of a loved one. Their efforts to find out every detail of his last hours are provoked by the inhuman and intolerable nature of this immediacy. Faced with the naked mystery of death, man endeavours to recover the warmer climate of dying, in order to feel the vital compassion that he needs. For this compassion enables one to feel closer to the departed by substituting the image of the dying man which still contains him in germ. To imagine a vital suffering, however atrocious the suffering may be, has in it something even relatively consoling. The act of dying in which the whole person may be concentrated, is an act essentially accessible to our understanding.[14] Life is our country, even when it is pain and compassion. In our sorrow we recover the personality of the dead man in the shape of his last act. Confronted by actual death, however, we seem banished from our own world. The impossibility of this vital sympathy, the impossibility of comprehending a person present, is the spiritual core of our suffering, or rather of this upheaval of our whole life which, it seems, only a religious faith can render tolerable. A living person is never entirely outside the range of our sympathy and understanding. This is

20

true even of someone who has died, perhaps many years ago at the other end of the earth, if only he lives again through the power of imagination. It is only through the experience of the death of another that we learn the qualitative nature of absence and separation. It sweeps away our soul into an unknown world, into a new dimension. We discover that our life is a bridge between two worlds.

The intensity of such experience may vary. It depends on the degree of one's own individualisation and the nature of the relationship between ourselves and the person of the dead. What is important above all, is the form of co-existence which is the background of the experience. The possibility of a change in our own being, considered as "being towards Death" (*Sein zum Tode*) which may follow the experience of the death of a fellow-creature, is based on the possibility of personal love. No-one would claim that the experience of the death of one's neighbour is the same as an experience of one's own death, which one has to meet: but its personal significance is so profound that it is an essential part of oneself, and not of the impersonal "one".[15] As a lived experience, it differs from the various psychic states it may include. It is in no sense a form of suffering and may even be received with a certain joy. To rejoice in the personal suffering of another is cruel, and to rejoice in a death struggle is diabolical. And where this vital sympathy is still human it includes pity. But, on the other hand, there is no such thing as feeling pity for death. Death causes no pain to the dead. The living may pity themselves, for what they have lost, but it is a form of suffering far removed from the vital pity we may feel for the dying.[16]

The sudden absence of the person as spirit may be interpreted in numerous different ways, particularly according to the differences inherent in the experience itself. Its fundamental content is never annihilation, but rather something like an open question. In this way the spirit may suffer far beyond what may properly be called pain. The greatest sufferings are not pain. To hold on to one's community with the dead is to preserve one's own existence - of which this community was an integral part - from destruction. The mind is therefore compelled to find a solution to the problem, a solution which always evades us, in order to allow the possibility of reconstituting the former community. Spiritual suffering is the suffering of enduring this terrible uncertainty, this complete lack of relationship, and the sense of abandonment and impotence. Compassion can form a bridge towards the other, and be thereby even a consolation. The doctrines of survival console the believer because they provide a concrete image of the dead and thus allow us to follow them at least in imagination, and sympathise with them. The various rites of burial give us the inestimable comfort of feeling that we can still do something for them, of having at our disposal ways of approaching their being. If it were only for this reason, Catholics would never abandon their belief in purgatory, a place where the existence of the dead and the state of their souls is still accessible to the charitable activity of the living.[17]

U The Ontological Basis

THE specifically human problem of death is created
by the transformation of the living being into *person*.
The problem becomes manifest in the history of
humanity, as in the biography of the individual, just in
so far as this fundamental transformation has taken
place. The person here is to be considered as an
existence that shapes itself; the actual form given to
the process of being-becoming (*Werdesein*) which
gives a meaning and a unity to the whole of an individual existence. The process has simply to appear,
to transform the whole of individuality into personality. All the elements which are present before personalisation lose their own intrinsic character through
this unifying transformation.[18] There is a specific relationship between this process of transformation that
is effected by the self-awareness of the person, and
a vital process which, *if isolated*, can be compared
with the vital processes in animals and plants. This
relationship is revealed in organic dissolution, one of
the characteristics of death. The organic process is,
in fact, of ambiguous significance in regard to the
shaping of the person. On the one hand, the organic
process, by its resistance, compels the person to
struggle for realisation ; on the other hand, it offers
the person the basis and the opportunity of realisation. And we might even say that, up to a certain
point, the data of physical existence are equally
transformable by personalisation. A unitary anthro-

pology which, in opposition to materialism, would incline towards a spiritual monism, might well be based on this fact. But the limits of this "angelic idealism" would be reached precisely at the point of human death. Here one would be confronted with an inevitable duality. Something in organic life evades personalisation.

The fulfilment of personal existence coincides only rarely with death ; and it is only in myth and dreams that the hero finds death as the culminating point of his perfection. From this face we may already conclude that death is not in its primitive sense an immanent possibility of personal existence, of the *Dasein* itself. Death comes from an alien sphere and is introduced as it were from outside into our existence. The spiritual appropriation of death is the supreme task of each human person, but the effort is an acknowledgment of the nature of this death which has to be transformed. Personal existence is not fatality; its task is to transform the fatality of death into liberty. The death of a man was originally similar to the death of a beast. Amongst primitive peoples there is still no great difference. It is only in connection with the progressive personalisation of the whole of human existence that it really acquires a new significance. The acceptance of death transforms death, but this very acceptance presupposes a resistance. The human person is not, in its true essence, an *existence towards death*. Like every other existence, after its own fashion, it is a movement towards self-realisation and towards eternity. It tends towards its own perfection, even if this means passing through the strait and narrow gate of death. It can only change its outer ontological aspect by turning death into the means of its own fulfilment. Metaphysics do not originate in the nothingness revealed by anguish, but in the being which by its very nature participates in the philosophic Eros. Thus the ontological character of the person is not derived from a negative which the person can only *accept*. The special decision through which the person may, in fact, become existence towards death, is an intermediate state between this primary exteriority of death, and the hope of the spirit, which transcends death itself.

The finality (*Unüberholbarkeit*) of death is only felt as suffering when the act which would have pointed towards survival and eternity has been swallowed up in despair. The anguish of death, and not only the pain of dying, would be incomprehensible if the fundamental structure of our being did not include the existential postulate of something beyond. Without this, death would simply be a future face, painful enough, no doubt, but without any exceptional gravity and without any danger of a metaphysical character. This very anguish reveals that death and nothingness are opposed to the deepest and most ineradicable tendencies of our being.[20] We are not speaking here of the instinct to duration, inherent in life in general, of Schopenhauer's will to live. At the very moment that I formulate the thought, I affirm the instinct in the human person ro realise and perpetuate itself. At the root of all being there is an act, the *affirmation of the self*. In each personality, aware of its uniqueness, we find the affirmation of this unique-

25

ness, moving towards its own realisation, an affirmation which implies the tendency to surpass the limits
of time. Faith in a personal survival is not merely a
comforting thought, it is above all the expression, the
actual shape given to this ontological factor. Death
considered as finality, physical death considered as
the universal negation of our existence, is only the
reflection of a despairing unbelief, a negation of the
person by the *person*. If human nature has need of a
belief in survival, this is neither egoism nor eccen-
tricity, nor some form of historical atavism. The very
need itself is witness to a fundamental state of being:
consciousness imitates the depth of being. If there
were no real possibility to correspond with this tendency, the whole of human existence would perish in
the abyss. Unamuno, who follows St. Paul in seeing
faith as "the substance of things hoped for" [20], redis-
covers in hope infinitely more than a human emotion.
Hope constitutes the meaning of our life and extends
the affirmation contained in the inmost core of being.
"For hope is the noblest fruit of the effort made by the
past to become the future, and it is this effort which
produces being, in the true sense of the word, and
gives it reality" [21]. A philosophy of existence which
denies the ontological foundation of the three human
virtues, is a philosophy against existence.[22]

Hope, this act of personal existence, is essentially
different from the multiple emotions which we can
describe as hope in the sense of the expectation of
something.[23] This does not mean that it lacks voli-
tional content. Hope does in fact possess a content,
but what it does not possess is a variable content,

precisely because it possesses its own incomparable inner content. It is a structure of being, transcending the psychic structure. Its content is immanent, and truly its own. This content exists only in hope and hope exists only in moving towards this content. Hope and expectation both appear to move towards the future. But there are two futures involved, appertaining to two kinds of time. The future of expectation is the future in the world in which one hopes for the fulfilment of certain desires. The future of hope is the future of my own person in which I shall fulfil myself. Hope is confidence in reaching towards the future and patience in the same act. Expectation has its roots in impatience, always anticipating its future and always doubting of itself. Hope tends, in principle, towards truth ; expectation, in principle, towards illusion.[24] Expectation admits a time which is of the world and of chance, hope creates a different time, which is of freedom and the person. Thus hope is in no sense an indeterminate aspect of expectation, a tendency of the soul to entertain varied expectations. It is determinate or indeterminate in a way peculiar to itself, according to the degree of clarity in its understanding of itself. Its opposite is not such and such a disappointment, but despair, which itself forms an indissoluble unity with its own content. Even if disappointment is generalised to become the sum of many disappointments, a state of mind to which the Spaniards give the term *desengaño*[25] this is not, in itself, despair, but a step in the purification of hope, which discovers its own meaning through transcending the world. Hope tends toward being, toward the actual, permanent and continuous shaping of the human person. Expectation anticipates through imagination, hope creates by giving structure to being. Expectation doubts, hope affirms, but it affirms by a creative movement of our whole existence.

In the same way, despair tends towards nothingness, whereas disappointment is only the painful destruction of imaginative anticipation. If we presume that without some instinct akin to hope the trees would not send forth new leaves in spring, we know that man, as a spiritual personality, cannot exist a single moment without hope. This is not the expectation of one thing or another, but a creative hope; the natural foundation of that hope of which it is written that "it maketh not ashamed." (*qu'elle ne nous laisse pas périr*).[26]

V I The Death of a Friend, according to the Fourth Book of the Confessions of St. Augustine

O monstrum vitæ et mortis profunditas!

IN the fourth book of his *Confessions* St. Augustine describes his experience of the death of one of his friends, as he felt it, at the time when he was professor of rhetoric at Tagaste, his place of birth, in Africa. During this period, whilst he was still, provisionally, a Manichæan, he lost a young friend who fell ill and died. The young man had been a fellow-student of his since boyhood, and was exceptionally dear to him although his name is not mentioned before the occasion of his untimely death. After having described the event, Augustine confesses to God the sorrow and misery into which he fell. He cannot confess this misery without analysing it, and he cannot embark on this analysis without immediately transcending the psychological element and arriving at something both more profound and more generalised. As, in his confession, he analyses the different states, not so much of his soul, as of his life, St. Augustine never fails to achieve an intuition of the metaphysical, the symbolic and the existential. He becomes Everyman to himself, and his *Confessions* are therefore the history of this Everyman.[27] In disclosing his own individual characteristics he transforms them into experience and in this sincere portrayal of his life he gives a faithful picture of the life and condition of man. The symbolic element has a generality which is immanent in reality itself. The story of the Confessions is the story of St. Augustine, a man who is like ourselves, and by this very fact it becomes the drama of the Everyman. The individual drama lights up the general drama. Speaking, for instance, of the theft of some pears, of which he was guilty in adolescence, St. Augustine provides us with a profound analysis of sin : speaking of the friend carried away by the spectacle of the circus and the gladiatorial combats, he gives us a powerful analysis of the dissolution of personal existence in the mass. "Everyman", says Montaigne, "carries in himself the whole of the human condition."

Thus, in this fourth book of the *Confessions*, which we are discussing at the moment, Augustine transcends the particular. I shall quote certain passages, which are really untranslatable, in as literal a translation as possible : [28] . . . "my heart was utterly darkened; and whatever I beheld was death. My native country was a torment to me, and my father's house a strange unhappiness ; and whatever I had shared with him, wanting him, became a distracting torture. Mine eyes sought him everywhere, but he was not granted them ; and I hated all places, for that they had not him ; nor could they now tell me, 'he is coming', as when he was alive and absent. I became a great riddle to myself, and I asked my soul, *why she was so sad, and why she disquieted me sorely* : but she knew not what to answer me. And if I said, *Trust in God*, she very rightly obeyed me not ; because that most dear friend, whom she had lost, was, being man, both truer and better, than that phantasm she was bid to trust in. Only my tears were sweet to me, for they succeeded my friend, in the dearest of my affections." [29]

Here we perceive all the elements of the death of the other, of which I have spoken. We see death operating as the present absence which transforms the whole world into death. "*Quidquid aspiciebam, mors erat.*" We grasp the radical difference between spatial and relative absence, on the one hand, and on the other, the final experience of absence felt at the death of the other. "*Expetebant eum undique oculi mei et non dabatur mihi; et oderam omnia, quia non haberunt eum, nec mihi jam dicere poterant. 'Ecce veniet', sicut cum viveret, quando absens erat.*" And immediately afterwards we can literally observe — and I am not exaggerating — the birth of existential philosophy : "I became a great riddle to myself — *Factus eram ipse mihi magna quaestio.*" Here is a questioning of being ; the philosophy of existence moving between hope and despair ; the philosophy through which man tries to understand his own condition. And he is necessarily brought to consider this question by the experience of the death of the other, since it reveals that man's mortal life cannot be taken to be his whole existence, nor existence itself. This struggle for hope which is part of the ontological quality of the human person, is revealed once more in St. Augustine. He says to his soul : "Hope in God". But this struggle cannot be victorious, since the God in whom the still Manichæan

31

Augustine believes, does not exist. We shall perhaps understand this fact better at the end of this essay. Thus there is only one consolation left to him, which involves a form of flight, and even of hypocrisy. He finds in his own tears the imaginary presence of the one whose loss he laments, which is now replaced by the lamentation itself. Augustine was given to tears, at all periods of his life, even on his deathbed. "*Requiescebam in amaritudine* — I . . . found my repose in bitterness", he says, a few lines later. Then he discovers the inner antinomy of his state : "*Et tœdium vivendi erat in me gravissimum et moriendi metus. Credo quo magis cum amabam, eo magis mortem quæ mihi abstulerat, tamquam atrocissimam inimicam oderam et timebam*". ". . . I loathed exceedingly to live, and feared to die. I suppose, the more I loved him, the more did I hate and fear, as a most cruel enemy, death, which had bereaved me of him." His problem had no solution, and despair was to be his constant companion, until he finds the God whom, as so often in the *Confessions*, he calls "my hope", *spes mea*. And finally, we find in these passages what we have called an existential participation, a "we" formed by the community between two persons, and we see how St. Augustine, by creating this "we", the product and the cornerstone of friendship, finds himself not only face to face with, but also, in some inexpressible manner, within the experience of his own death. "For I wondered that others, subject to death, did live, since he whom I loved, as if he should never die, was dead : and I wondered yet more that myself, who was to him a second self, could live, he being dead. Well said one of his friend, 'Thou half of my soul' : for I felt that my soul and his soul were 'one soul in two bodies' : and therefore was my life a great horror to me, because I would not live halved." [30] Thus he had entrusted his personal existence to this community with a friend, and now the tragic infidelity and flight of this friend uproots his personal life : "I had remained to myself a hapless spot, where I could neither be, nor be from thence."[31] It took many years for this disquiet to become prayer and confession, and thus lead to the victory of hope, the hope which finally attains awareness of itself.

The text of the *Confessions* is inexhaustible. I must now leave it with regret, to take up, somewhat ashamedly, my own analyses of the diversity, particularly the historic diversity, of the experience of death. If I write of various doctrines belonging to the history of philosophy, it should be understood that this is in order to arrive at an analysis of certain experiences which, in their essential content, belong neither to a school nor to an epoch. The possibility of fundamental human experience underlies all authentic philosophy.

VII The Forms of Experience of Death

THE general outline of the attitude of the human person towards the problem of death, as we have tried to define it, shows that the sense of our mortality, which derives from the experience of death, naturally acquires a very different meaning according to the manner in which we formulate the dependence or independence of personal life on bodily-life.

We anticipate something of the specific character of our own death in each experience which speaks to us of this fundamental relationship. In some forms of experience we feel our personality being trammelled, shattered or stifled by our corporeality. Here death appears to us as the destruction of the person itself. The person seems to be only the smoke of the vital fires fed by the hard and solid reality of the living body. If at such a moment we visualise the corporeal reality of our life as destroyed, the person must also appear annihilated and dissolved, since now it will apparently lack its own central force. Man, in such a state, is the prey to an unlimited anguish of death, which is quite different from a vital fear. And the whole spirit of the person is concentrated in this anguish. It is the horror of the person at the prospect of metaphysical abandonment, an abandonment that is already present in an anticipation of the end of corporeal existence. The prison house was also a shelter. Man has no confidence in his powers of resistance to isolation and thus he is, as it were, annihilated in anticipation. However, even here this anticipatory anguish is never entirely without hope, or without a belief in survival ; it is, however, weak, a negative belief in survival, in a passivity which is dissolution. It is survival without weight and without energy, like the Homeric survival, worse than the life of a slave, and which disappears in the tedium of a mortal isolation. Death as an absolute end is an empty concept which we do not experience, even in the anguish of death. The form of experience I have just mentioned may be found in any of those states of mind in which the corporeal, psycho-physical life is considered as active and dominant, and the purely personal spiritual life as dependent and passive. This depreciation of the spirit may be effected as much through pleasure as through pain. This is the chief reason why in pleasure we are so close to a mortal tedium and to the anguish of death. When death suddenly enters in upon the rejoicings of the flesh, it seems to prolong the diversion, the *motus defectivus* of the person towards nothingness, the *motus* by which man flees from the deepest law of his being.

In direct opposition to this type of experience, are those states in which we are aware of the true activity of our personal existence. Then we are able to overcome this anguish and inner tedium. We feel that death may set free a force which seems able to exist independently of corporeal life. Such experiences, which may be called ecstatic - in the broadest sense of the word - are not exclusive to religious life, but may arise from any state of profound spirituality. Ever since Plato, the philosophers of the spirit have followed this path in order to justify by argument the hope of survival. Their arguments barely veil a fundamental experience. The most recent of them, Max Scheler, argues from the autonomy of spiritual acts in relation to the vital process. Our acts of cognition, for instance, are not necessarily subject to a biological determination. They are, on the contrary, shaped "by the very nature of the thing", by the actual essence of the content towards which our intention of cognition is directed. Thus, in every real act of cognition, man participates not only in the object but also at the same time in a supra-vital order which must be inaccessible to death. This concept must finally result in the platonic doctrine of the superiority of philosophy over death. It is derived from a position which has itself its origin in the actual experience of the autonomy of the spiritual personality. In a philosophic rapture man may see physical death as something beneath him, something vile and impotent. Philosophy itself becomes an anticipation of death, a personal act of dying, a partial realisation of physical death before its fatal intervention. The socratic or platonic philosopher may in this way give expression to spiritual immortality in this life itself. The real subject of the *Phædo*, which is surely much more convincing than the logical proofs of immortality which it provides, is the life and hope and the way of dying of Socrates himself. In Plato these doctrines do go far beyond the orphic elements which can be distinguished in his writings. Here we find a real living, a lived philosophy, which forms the very core of the Dialogues. [32] For instance, in Plato, the idea of the body as the prison house of the soul is not only the repetition of an established orphic theme, but an expression of the philosophic act itself, which by transcending the body transforms the meaning of life and death. Victory over death does not in this case proceed from any quality of man in general, but appears as part of the concent of hope; it is the result of that inner activity which is true philosophy. But the successful outcome of this activity can only be assured by the philosophic encounter with a world which exists independently of man, and which is, by its nature, outside mortality. Man's quality of eternity is achieved through participation, and this participation is the essence of all true cognition. The autonomy of the spirit in relation to life and death depends on the extent to which man participates in the world of ideas. All participation is a transformation of the participant and cognition itself is this transformation of the human subject. To philosophise is to die; it is to leave the world of images, the cave of shadows, for another world which is truly existent, since it is eternally present — it is to leave the world, not in a spatial sense, but literally in the sense of the transformation of being, which is inherent in the philosophic act itself.

Let us return for a moment to the experience of anguish ; the quasi-inexistence of the spirit of the dead man was due to the fact that the spirit lacked any basis for being present once it was deprived of body and isolated from the world of the living. The expatriated spirit assumed the nature of a *spectre*, of something with an existence not entirely to be denied but which seems somehow to be lacking, since it does not admit the idea of the possibility of a true presence. [33] Spirit can only exist in community. If we wish to conceive of an autonomy of the spirit sufficiently powerful to reach beyond death, then we need to believe that spirit is not isolated in death but at least introduced into another world. Isolation [34] is not compatible with the inner structure of personal existence and implies the tendency to annihilation. Thus the spectre remains in a dubious relationship to the world to which it no longer belongs. Thus the platonic attitude to death is only possible if one admits the ontology of ideas. But this also introduces us to the fundamental limitations of Platonism. The spiritual world with which the spirit of the dead man will now co-exist, in which it will participate by taking on the form of existence proper to this new world, is still only a world of ideas. Is the person itself to become an idea ? This spirit-person would then be a transitory and secondary form of the spirit which, in its own essence, would be idea. Here we are confronted with an antinomy, for man's survival must be personal if it is to be the survival that his hope leads him to seek, the sole survival worthy of the name. On the other hand, the ontology of ideas themselves is inevitably obscure unless they are understood to be secondary forms of the spirit, as it were, products of a person. The world brought to us by the ancient philosophers is not a *world of neighbours*, a world shaped by *caritas*; it is, above all, a world of things, a world of things seen, and even men are such things, public, limited beings. The transcendental world reflects the character of the empirical world. It is like the world of ideas, which are things seen by the spirit, and not like the world of persons. [35]

The ontology of ideas is still dependent on the ontology of nature ; it has not yet reached the full clarity of categories of mind. This is not a criticism of Plato's doctrines, but it is impossible not to perceive the limits of his experience. The philosopher seems to have been acutely aware of this himself, and appears, for this reason, to have left unsolved the difficulties created by the interpretation of the existence of the world of ideas. His limitations are the limitations of all pre-Christian philosophy in Europe. The *person* was not yet disclosed, and the sense of death remained hidden. Man was still in process of discovering the spiritual world of philosophic thought. He had become aware of abstract concepts, but he had not yet become aware of himself as person, through the spontaneous manifestation of the person as the eternal, primordial existence of the spirit.

This limitation of the platonic ascension explains why those periods of philosophic thought which were to some extent influenced by the Academy, as well as the Academy itself, which fell into scepticism, did not retain the concept of the supra-natural quality of ideas, and thus lost touch with the platonic initiation into death and immortality. It would be necessary to review the history of philosophy from Aristotle up to the triumph of Christianity, in order to follow the long meditation on death which was the vital core of their preoccupations. This period of increasing individualisation was dominated perhaps more exclusively than any other by the concept of death. Let us consider the traditions which typified two forms of experience; the tradition of Epicurus and the tradition of the Stoa.

Epicurus is the originator of a doctrine which has been repeated and discussed at infinite length. It might be called the sophism of the inexistence of death. Diogenes Laertius is quoting Epicurus [36] when he says that death is nothing, as far as we are concerned. If we exist, death does not yet exist: if death exists, we no longer exist. Cicero has popularised this sophism.[37] But the commentary provided by Lucretius is the most illuminating : "Do you not know that death will not leave you another self which will live to stand and weep over your corpse?" [38] Indeed, if all reality resides in the sensations, death does not concern me, since when I am dead, I shall be incapable of feeling my death. The sole problem that remains is to find the most comfortable way of dying, which tradition claims that Epicurus himself achieved by drinking wine in a hot bath. It is fairly easy to demonstrate the type of experience which underlies this doctrine. It is derived on the one hand from the fact that all vital suffering ends, even in the spectator, at the moment of death, and on the other from the still more obvious fact of the insensitivity of the corpse. But the conclusion remains a sophism, and is only a formula of escape. It endeavours to disprove verbally something from which man cannot escape in reality, the complete upheaval of human existence, not through fear of any disagreeable sensation which might be experienced after death, but by an anguish at the thought of death itself and its power over the person. The epicurean argument is current every-where in the eclectic philosophy of the period. Even Seneca, the Stoic, makes use of it, adding an impor-tant comment: "What is extreme is not bad. Has death come to you? It would be indeed terrible if death were to stay. But it is inevitable that it should either not come at all, or having come, depart imme-diately."[39] If we look at this last sentence, it would seem that Seneca has not entirely grasped the dis-tinction made by Epicurus between dying and death; but his words retain all the flavour of the sensuality and subjectivity of epicurean thought.

We are also indebted to Seneca for a particularly clear interpretation of the stoic doctrines of death as we find them, for instance, in Epictetus and Marcus Aurelius. These doctrines seem peculiarly character-istic of a state of mind which was very widespread amongst cultured circles during the Roman Empire. To the Stoic, death was part of the ordered "All" of the "Cosmos" in the same way as birth. "You are brought back to your source." [40] It is a general law which is inevitable and applies to all and is therefore just. It should occasion neither astonishment nor complaint. But death is not an absolute end, since man belongs to a Cosmos which can only fulfil its own great law and achieve the fulness of its existence through the death of individuals. Nothing in the world is lost - "Things cease to be, but do not perish." [41] But we can only grasp the true significance of such thinking if we understand it as the actual outcome of an unceasing endeavour to ensure the supremacy of the individual over death. "In order never to fear death, think of it

41

unceasingly." [42] This supremacy, which would imply the total and decisive triumph of reason over the passions - and thus over destiny - is the whole purpose and wisdom, the whole virtue and felicity of the stoic way of living. The passions to be controlled are the instinctive clinging to life and the instinctive horror of death. The philosopher is seeking a state of mind in which man, through the power of reason, the use of meditation, and the profound conviction that death is not an evil in itself, shall have so diminished these instincts that he can decide with a tranquil mind whether he himself shall live or die. "Take control of that which is under the control of another." [43] We must make death our own in order to free ourselves from it. [44] If a situation should arise to provide rational motives for dying, man should be in a state of mind which allows him to choose death freely, and to end his life calmly, coldly, and with unshakable purpose.[45]

Stoicism is essentially a doctrine of freedom, and this freedom is based on the possibility of a choice of death. But this choice of death is not, of course, to be confused in any way with suicide which, in the majority of cases, is only the effect of passion, and therefore, for a Stoic, the depth of servitude. Thus it is not so much a question of the reality, but of the possibility of making this free choice of death — of a certain attitude of mind already achieved. This attitude, this psychological possibility, is only to be found in the *virtus moriendi* [46] which is the very essence of wisdom. As for the objective possibility, this is a gift of God for which the Stoics frequently express their gratitude. A door is open by which man can escape from all servitude. "What is evil is to live in necessity; but there is no necessity to live in necessity. Why no necessity? Because a path to freedom is open on every side. The ways are countless, short and easy. Let us thank God that no one can be forced to remain alive." [47] Man must learn to be able to die, in order to imitate, if necessary, the glorious example of Socrates and Cato. [48] The wise man is revealed by his manner of dying and his manner of awaiting death. "Death will pass judgment on you."[49] The man who dies without any fear or anguish, either a natural death, or at the hands of the executioner, or by his own hand, proves that he has fulfilled his task in life, that he has achieved in his own self the sovereignty of reason according to the order of the Cosmos. If the sophism of Epicurus is a subtle ruse to escape - if not from death, at least from the concept of death and an obsession with death - this other doctrine, more akin to the heroism of Cato, is not without a certain too deliberate bravura. The Stoic looks closely at death, in spite of what La Rochefoucauld says, but even if he goes unflinchingly to meet it, is there not an immense experience of anguish underlying this desperate action of the will? We have examples displaying the two extremes of this contempt for death, from Lucian's story of Peregrinus Proteus and his caricature of suicide, to the heroic gesture of a young poet of our own times, Lauro de Bosis. [50] In Seneca, this deliberate action derives from the need to diminish the importance of death. In Seneca's hands the epicurean argument has become the very means of securing a stoic liberation. The old man who writes to

43

Lucilius cannot abandon any of his defences against the menace of death. I find Epictetus wiser, with his almost inhuman calm. While Marcus Aurelius is in fact inconsolable in his melancholy. The stoic experience is an experience of the courage which gives us a foundation of hope which persists even when there are no longer any grounds for hope, which persists because we are ourselves hope before we become despair, but a foundation which can never of itself totally eliminate despair. The stoic decision is not an escape as with the Epicureans; it is an attack which includes an element of despair. However, the stoic attitude seems to me to be the noblest that can be achieved if we do not accept that man participates in an order of existence which transcends death. This transcendental order is to some extent replaced in the stoic philosophy by the pantheistic concept of the All, the Cosmos — by the immanence of universal reason. The stoic philosophy was thus able to establish, in its grave and lucid manner, a concept of the true way of dying and the means of achieving it, due, no doubt, to a perfection of pagan thought, which is deeply and consciously tragic, and which has found disciples in every age, particularly since the Renaissance. The stoic solution did therefore carry a real power. Yet this marriage of reason and death conveys a note of hesitation, and never finds the authentic accent of the victory of hope over death, an accent which, in the centuries before Christ, was exclusive to the Mysteries, and particularly to the philosophic Mystery of Platonism.

VIII Intermezzo in the Bull Ring

THE life of a man without God is much like a tragedy, if one considers its structure and its end, and not any one of its isolated moments. It is difficult to visualise this total picture. We can grasp it by analogy if we become aware of the symbolic meaning of that survival of the Mysteries known as the Bull fight. Paganism is essentially melancholy, and only the promise of eternity and resurrection can justify the affirmation of hope which is at the core of human existence.

The bull that enters the arena knows nothing of what awaits him. He rushes joyfully from the obscurity of his prison and rejoices in the vitality of his youthful powers. Dazzled by the sudden light he feels himself master of the closed circle which becomes his world and which still seems to him a boundless plain. He tosses up the sand of the arena and rushes in every direction, with no other sensation than that of joy in his own power. — Thus the infant leaves the body of his mother and soon begins to play in a luminous world which still conceals his destiny and its attendant dangers.

The first adversaries enter the ring. It is still a game. Combat is natural to the bull. The struggle intensifies his awareness of life and of his own strength. These little vexations at the beginning merely build up his anger. It is the rage of the strong which reaches full measure in this provocation. The struggle calls forth the attacking animal which lay hidden beneath his everyday existence. There is nothing disagreeable beyond the limits of the game. But slowly a painful element is introduced. The game is rigged. The adversary is too cunning, he provokes and then retreats. Although the weaker of the two, the adversary becomes the stronger, because he is bad. The redness of the cloth becomes exasperating; it is no longer the happy pretext for a fight.

Thus the adolescent at school and elsewhere has his first encounters with a guileful world against which the sincerity of his struggle is unavailing. But the fatigue of youth is not important.

The fight only becomes serious for the bull with the entry of his enemies on horseback. From high above him the picadors strike at him with their lances and wound him from a distance. The bull attacks: he surpasses himself in his fury. His rage is now magnificent, blind and suffering; its frenzy secretly inspired by a despair of life, but constantly reinforced by a perpetual victory over this despair. It is the innocent old horse which suffers worst from his stubborn attack. The wily picador disappears when his bloody task is completed. — So does man enter on the real struggle of his life. He can never overcome evil. If he destroys any one of his adversaries, he will only have destroyed an innocent. Here all are innocent ; our adversaries are only masks for the Evil which we shall never destroy.

At this moment the bull is still strong. But from now on his reserves are failing. He looks stronger than he really is. His grip on life is shaken. The wounds from the lances were deep and his blood is flowing. And now the action is held up by an intermezzo. He is to be decorated, and also wounded again. There is both respect and mockery in festooning this gallant fighter with bandilleros. And the heroic beast provides an almost comic pretext for the elegant dance of the bandillero, the man who garlands him with these lethal darts, and succeeds in planting his weapon, in spite of his own fears, thanks to the very grandeur and slowness of the driven bull. — Thus man in his maturity attains honour and success at the very moment when he is weakened by the wounds of life. And even worldly glory is only a more secret wound, a traditional and almost ridiculous decoration, a travesty of victory. For he has conquered nothing. No one is victor in this world. We pretend that he has been victorious, as if true glory lay at the disposal of man. This is indeed an insult. [51] The bull, at least, does not believe in his new honours. Perhaps he has even the foreboding that the world only glorifies those whom it is about to sacrifice.

Then with the matador [52], the high priest of the mystery, death enters the arena. Behold it! It is the sword, beautiful, supple and inevitable, hidden under the terrible red of the cloth, but hidden only from the one destined to receive it. The others behold this death, and the weakened bull enters his agony, and in transcending this agony reaches a deeper, though not yet ultimate gravity after the tragi-comedy of the interlude. The tragedy begins, or rather the tragic significance of the whole spectacle is finally disclosed. A good bull remains dignified, a fighter to the end.

I do not think that he still believes in victory. But though almost without intelligence, he is not without an obscure awareness of the approaching moment, an awareness which has been brusquely sharpened by the adventures of the past twenty minutes, which comprise a lifetime. There have been struggles and attacks, withdrawal and return, on both sides. There has been success and defeat. The combat has not rested on a purely physical plane. The matador, summoning up his will, tries to lead and dominate the bull, manœuvering him into the only position which will allow of a mortal blow. He waves the red flag of death, so that it masters the bull, compelling him to follow it, like a lover dying beneath the spell of a supreme mistress. And suddenly the bull is killed. His massive body wears the sword like a last proud cry of despair. For a few seconds he seems to resist. But death comes, the death that has so long been present, identified with the sword, and identical with its source, the matador who wields it. The dead animal is carried away, like a thing. — Thus we all come to death in this world. Every battle with death is lost before it begins. The splendour of the battle cannot lie in its outcome, but only in the dignity of the act. The definitive is the inevitable.

In the bull ring the bull takes the place of man and man plays the role of the archangel or demon. He revenges himself for being in the grip of fate by taking on the role of fate towards another. For once it is man who knows and foresees what he will accomplish. Thus for two hours he can forget his own inevitable death by becoming master of the death of

a substitute. Within the limitations of a purely immanent concept of the nature of human life and death,
there is no mystery with a higher symbolic content
than this. For once man can feel that he is the victor
by allying himself with the invincible enemy. But in
the depths of his soul he knows that he is the bull,
that the superhuman stoicism of the matador is fictitious and that this struggle, with so tragically predes-
tined an outcome, is his own. [53] Yet all the same, man
does not despair in the face of truth; yet his hope can
never be complete unless there should be, after all,
the possibility of a victory over death. Man never
despairs entirely so long as he is alive but — the certainty of a possible victory can only be found in
Christianity.

IX The Christian Experience of Death

WE have now come to the interpretation of the Christian experience of death and here I wish to deal particularly with a type of mystical experience. It is far from easy to explain the way in which I wish to treat this subject, which can no longer be postponed, nor, indeed, by what right I deal with it at all. When speaking of the death of a friend, as a human experience, common to "everyman", all I needed to do was to evoke and explore an experience I had had myself, and such as the reader may have experienced. But now it is a question of an experience which is not only very specific, historically speaking, but extremely rare and of a special character. I have myself had no experience of such kind, although sometimes I have the impression that I am very slowly beginning to understand those mystics who bear witness to us, before God, that they have undergone this experience. I shall therefore limit myself to quoting from certain documents which are within the bounds of comprehension of those who, like myself, are not mystics, and I shall try, for our better understanding, to interpret them as best I can. Naturally anyone is free to treat these documents as the purely psychological material produced by a special type of mentality which has, somehow or other, to be explained. One is also free to accept that here we find the most intimate and authentic experience, therefore the rarest and most incommunicable that can be

achieved by man. As a philosopher I am not compe-
tent to pronounce on such exceptional experiences,
where nothing can be proved. One can only describe
and interpret very modestly. Everyone is free, logi-
cally free, to make what he can of them. As for
myself, I admit that I believe that they contain the
truth of the mystery : "*0 monstrum vitæ et mortis profunditas.*"

Christ brings to the believer an entirely new liberation from death. He fulfils the foreshadowings of
Platonism and the Mysteries by revealing a realm of
the spirit which is inaccessible to death, a realm in
which man may participate. In this new religion man
may transform and transcend his mortal condition
since beyond death there is a possibility of life, the
only life worthy of the name, since its condition is
eternity. There is a possibility of a life for human persons alongside the Divine, so close to the Divine that
the human partakes of its eternity. In all Christian
thought we find this same dialectic of death which
expresses the real change in the human situation
caused by the appearance and example of Christ.

Earthly life is mortal life. [54] Such is the temporal
nature of this life that no real presence can occur in
it. The world disintegrates at every moment. The
moment dies as it is born. The past devours the
future before any present existence can be achieved
in duration. The moment, the only place and the only
earthly opportunity of being present, thus the only
possible opportunity of existence, slips away through
time into time. "*Ex illo quod nondum est, per illud
quod spatio caret, in illud quod jam non est.*" (From

that which is not, through that which has no dimension, into that which no longer exists.) [55] There is no *time*, there are only *three times* and these three inseparable aspects *sunt in anima tria quaedam*, are a part of the soul. They correspond to the three faculties of the soul : *memoria, contuitus, exspectatio*, i.e. memory, intuition and expectation. The analysis of time which St. Augustine gives us in the eleventh book of his Confessions, although it is strongly influenced by Plotinus, is unique in the philosophy of Europe. It is above all an ontological analysis of the terrestrial world as characterised by its temporality, as well as an analysis of its metaphysical constitution.

The unquiet soul leads us ever towards the future, thus creating the past at every moment by immediately abandoning the present. This disquiet and this instability form not only the basis of our sense of time, but also vitiate the constitution of the world as world, (*sæculum*) at its very root, and thus create a mobility of time. Time, by seeming to move from the past through the present towards the future, *this time is ourselves*, in so far as we do not participate in eternity, the eternity which is both stability and pure presence and identical with God. It is intention that makes eternity ; whereas the *distensio* of the human soul marks the transition from the pure and lasting presence of eternity to the mortal time of this world, by a diminution in being. Thus mortality arises from the depth of our disquiet, this mortality which is our most peculiarly personal characteristic, both immanent and perpetual, the fruit and punishment of sin.

We cannot exist as persons at any moment of our life without on the one hand remembering, mainly with regret, nor on the other, without looking forward with fresh hope. Man is separated at each instant from something, because at each instant he moves forward to a fresh encounter. Each particle of temporal life contains both death and the tendency to fight against death. "*So leben wir und nehmen immer Abschied.*" [56] Christian time — as Saint Augustine interprets it — is the time of the soul which seeks its own existence in seeking God. "*Quia fecisti nos, ad te et inquietum est cor nostrum donec requiescat in te!*"

Heraclitus, Plato and the Platonists had already reflected on the evanescence of this world, and had provided an ontological interpretation which is similar though more objective. But for the Christian there is not only a world of ideas in the sphere of eternity, but also a person, who is absolute being, a person who, by Grace allowing man to share His eternity, may determine the transformation of man by the free and boundless love that is manifest in the Incarnation.

Man's participation in the eternity of the Divine can only achieve total realisation beyond death, and in such a way that death itself becomes a form of birth superior to empirical birth. If there is a life which is really death, there is a death which is in truth Life. [57] Then damnation appears as the only true death, the only eternal death, since it is the final exclusion from the source of Life, the decisive loss of the possibility of such a participation. The saints who die in being born into the beatific vision, attain the Life eternal, the divine presence which is the only real presence. The spiritual person of the dead is not annihilated, it acquires its final existence in death or in life, in Hell or in Heaven. The righteous attain the participation of being ; the damned suffer death with the devil, who has himself only a false immortality, since death is his condition. [58] Lucifer goes on dying to infinity — through not dying with Christ, in the same way as the Wandering Jew of the legend dies, slowly, but not to infinity.

This dialectic should be of interest to us here because it corresponds to the reality of Christian experience and sheds a most revealing light on the revolution in values it entails. This dialectic is an explanation and an extension of the Christian way of living, just as the platonic dialectic was an extension and an explanation of the philosophy initiated by Socrates and continued by the Academy. For the strength of the Christian promise is also derived from lived experience. Empirical death can, in fact, begin in the midst of life with mortification, with methods which partially liberate the soul from the body and the promptings of the body ; but at the same time, by the Grace of God, true Life, eternal Life, can to a certain degree become present here below. Saint Thomas Aquinas speaks of an *inchoatio vitæ æternæ*. There is an initial transformation which seems to result in a conversion [59] of the human attitude and human emotions towards death. The anguish of death seems to be transformed into an anguish of mortal life, of life without God, and attachment to terrestrial life seems to entail an empirical death if it is to be transcended.

Man only flees one form of death, whilst seeking a different form at the same time. From the moment of conversion all that is important is to know "how to die", death becoming the pathway to a true life, the pathway to the perfection of the *inchoatio*. This conversion occurs to a greater or less degree in all those who are sincerely trying to become Christians, and can of course never, or perhaps hardly ever, be complete. But the beginning of this conversion is usually only brought about by faith. There are very few in whom this faith is immediately followed by a "*cognitio experimentalis*", by an immediate spiritual experience. The experience of God which is granted to mystics includes an experience of death which is peculiar to them. They are in no sense superior to other believers ; neither are they monsters or paradoxical exceptions to the religious life. But owing to one of the multiple activities of Grace, they have a special access to the same mysteries. But if we are looking for the profoundest expression of the human experience of death, their spirituality is more important to us than that of the saints who were heroes of faith and obedience. But although this discrimination is justified in principle it is liable to be too intransigent if it is immediately applied to human reality. "*Credo ut intelligam.*" If it is true to say that there is no Christian mysticism outside the bounds of the common faith, it is also true that there is no saint who has been entirely without mystical experience. Christian mysticism is first of all one form of Christian life, and not an experience of a "mystical character", a category which might include the most diverse forms of fanaticism and emotionalism. Deism and pantheism have been guilty of vast errors in accepting whatever was warm and friendly and elementary in man's emotional life as being equivalent to a religious life. If mystical phenomena occur in the various revealed religions, that is to say, if there is an experience of the content of their revelation, the analogy which exists between these phenomena is rather an analogy of form and expression than an analogy of spirit. [60] And this difference between the form and its spiritual content becomes of cardinal importance when we are speaking of the "ineffable". The hideous medley of Plotinus, Master Eckhart, Buddha and St. Theresa that we sometimes meet, is due exclusively to a lack of clarity and an almost complete absence of any feeling for spiritual realities in many modern writers. Let us therefore begin by accepting that it is the Christian life in all its forms which underlies the conversion of man's attitude with regard to death.

On the threshold of Christian mysticism stands St. Augustine, perhaps the greatest theoretician of the mystic life the West has ever known, and a writer who, apart from the Gospels, has had the greatest influence on the language of all Western mysticism. But it is still a question as to whether he was a mystic himself. There is not sufficient evidence in the period prior to the *Confessions* to allow us to reach any conclusions, whereas the period covered by this book is characterised by two experiences of a clearly mystical nature. The first constitutes the decisive moment of conversion, the moment in the garden in Milan (*Conf.*, VIII, 12). The second experience occurs at Ostia Tiberina, shortly after his conversion. It is the culminating point of his long contemplation of God, an experience which he had shared in spiritual unity with his mother, St. Monica. There is something momentous and exceptional, even paradoxical about these two experiences which make them outstanding in his life. At the time when, in the *Confessions*, he makes his confession of faith, he is not a mystic, he has only some vague comprehension of the possibility of the mystic life. Let us compare the passage dealing with the moment at Ostia Tiberina with that other passage describing the state of his soul during the period of the *Confessions*. Here is the moment at Ostia Tiberina : [61] "(. . . and in swift vision touched [62] on that Eternal Wisdom, which abideth over all) — could this be continued on, and other visions of kind far unlike be withdrawn, and this one ravish and absorb, and wrap up its beholder amid these inward joys, so that life may be for ever like that one moment of understanding which now we sighed after ; were not this, 'Enter into thy Master's joy' ?" And here is the other passage, from the time of the *Confessions*, towards the end of the tenth book which gives us the *contuitus* of his life at that time : "And sometimes Thou admittest me to an affection, very unusual, in my inmost soul ; rising to a strange sweetness, which if it were perfected in me, I know not what in it would not belong to the life to come. But through my miserable encumbrances I sink down again into these lower things, and am swept back by former custom, and am held, and greatly weep, but am greatly held. So much doth the burthen of a bad custom weigh us down. Here I can stay, but would not ; there I would, but cannot ; both ways, miserable." Miser utrobique![63]

No-one could provide a clearer, more exact description of this level of spiritual life than is given by St. Augustine in his heroic simplicity. It is a state of the Christian soul which is bordering on the mystical vision without being able to enter it. It is the life of hope, developed and shaped by hope, the theologal virtue, hope not yet fulfilled, though indeed consoled, and yet at the same time intensified, by all that it still contains of disquiet. Immediately after the moment at Ostia, there enters the experience of the death of the other, an experience which reveals the same state of duality, but one that is already quite different from that form of hopelessness which he had felt at the death of his childhood friend. Now it is his mother who dies — his mother who was, as it were, his mediator, his symbol of Grace. St. Monica's death was fully and joyfully Christian, but it discloses the struggle still being fought out in St. Augustine's heart. In the twelfth and following chapters of Book 9 he talks of this experience which occurred after the union of mother and son in mystical contemplation. St. Augustine says that a death like that of his mother should have been to him a source of deepest joy instead of overwhelming him with all too human sorrow : "*Illa nec misere moriebatur, nec omnino moriebatur,*" (she died neither miserably, nor totally). Should he not be convinced that here is neither misery nor annihilation ? *Omnimoda extinctio*, total extinction, he writes. Why does he therefore weep in solitude, hiding from the friends who are chanting the funeral psalms ? He explains his motive, a very human and natural one — the same that had induced his utter misery at the death of his friend in Tagaste : "*Quoniam itaque deserebar tam magno eius solatio, sauciabatur anima mea, et quasi dilaniabatur vita, quæ una facta erat ex mea et illius.*" "Being then forsaken of so great comfort in her, my soul was wounded, and that life rent asunder, as it were, which, of hers and mine together, had been made but one." [64] Once more we find in these pages the signs of the emotional disturbance which is produced by the severance of the terrestrial links in a community of souls. And yet Augustine is no longer a Manichæan but a Christian. Hope in God will prove stronger than his sadness, and misery will not long remain an element in his recollections of his saintly mother. In the depth of his soul despair is from this point overcome.

This is why St. Augustine is unmistakably established at the centre of Christian life, in the human sense, for he is only on the threshold of the specifically mystic life. But in order to give some idea of what the experience of death can be at the highest peak of Christian living, I must quote another example. This concerns the spiritual sister of St. Monica, St. Theresa of Avila, who says herself in her *Life* that she felt she could recognise her own portrait in the *Confessions*, but who seems nevertheless to have gone further along the mystic way than was possible for the essentially virile dualism of the son.

The idea of death acquires, as it were, more of a vibrant hue, in the souls of the mystics, because with them their love of death proceeds from a direct experience of a state analogous to death. This experience is the anticipation, in ecstasy, of death. It was said of St. Theresa that she "swam in the supernatural like a fish in water." [65] This also marks the essential difference between her and St. Augustine. I quote a passage from Chapter 38 of her *Life*, which seems particularly characteristic. "I felt little of that fear of death which I had always felt so intensely. Now it seemed to me the easiest possible thing to the soul that serves God, since, in a moment, it is liberated from prison and set at rest. This raising up of the spirit towards God, who shows it such excellent things in these ravishments, seemed to me very similar to the moment when the soul entirely leaves the body and finds itself at once in the fulness of this Good." [66]

There is thus in the first place a slow conversion of the quite natural human attitude to death into its opposite, and secondly a clear and decisive relationship, by analogy, between this conversion and the experience of the ecstatic order, called "ravishment". In these ravishments St. Theresa suffers first of all an indescribable pain, followed immediately by a still more excessive sweetness. The first moment is similar to that in which the soul is separated from the body and from the world : the second moment, the moment of calm, is analogous to the presence of God in the beatific vision. The first moment suggests the bitterness of death, the second announces life eternal. Throughout the whole of the *Life* one can in this way follow every stage of the conversion of the sense of death. Finally her prayer was to be : "*Señor, o morir or padecer*" (Lord either to die or to suffer).

The sense of the presence of the existence of God had so driven out her sense of earthly realities, that in spite of her activities as a reasonable and saintly woman, she lived a sort of dream in life, "*una manera de sueño en la vida*", thinking that what she saw with the eyes of the body was a dream. After her vision of the angel whom she felt pierce her heart with his flaming staff, she began sometimes to see the dead in their glory. Then she saw her pious parents and St. Peter of Alcantara. Eternal life seemed to have invaded this life in time, and the butterfly wished to emerge from the prison of the caterpillar. [67]

Thus St. Theresa speaks of the analogy between "ravishment" and birth into eternal life with such clarity that even we others who are not mystics can attain a certain understanding. If she really wished for death during the last phase of her life, it was not simply because she had had enough of life. A woman with such a prodigious gift for activity was incapable of feeling the *ennui* of those who see no tasks to be accomplished here below. She was not a melancholic. The melancholic may wish for death because life is painful to him. There are "born suicides" who suffer, not from such and such a way of living, but from life itself. The mystic, however, suffers from life mainly because he is in love with death or, more strictly speaking, with something contained in death. The sweetness of birth into a new life seems to him to be infinitely stronger than the pain which still characterises the separation from earthly life. Thus it is not solely because the mystic holds firmly and eagerly to the promise of eternal beatitude that he awaits

61

the arrival of his last hour with impatience. He has already known this beatitude. St. Theresa believed that she had participated in this higher life — by analogy, since it was not eternal — that she had participated for a few instants in that which she hoped to attain through a final liberation. There is thus nothing morbid in her desire for death, and it infinitely surpasses the stoic calm and the platonic ascension. Indeed, man cannot love death for the sake of death. He can only love death if it is transformed into a state which is no longer death. A true love of death can only be a form of the love of God. Death is then the last fulfilment of the mystic marriage of God and the soul. The love in the soul, that force which decides its real presence, has already moved away from the world. Death offers the soul a community with the eternal lover as its permanent state. It offers the soul a community with the One who is and who gives being, the One whom St. Theresa has felt gradually approaching in those moments of sober and superhuman intoxication during her earthly life. In ravishment itself the mortal pain is only a prelude to a boundless joy. This joy, in so far as it is feeling, indicates the act by which being is affirmed. It is the fulfilment of the ontological hope, through something else which, not derived from hope, comes to complete it. Man, as a person, feels himself becoming, through the action of Grace, what he is in God. He is at last aware of being, and understands that before he was nothingness ; that he was nothing but an unfulfilled hope. Spiritual joy is only a reflection of a movement towards being. It is thus possible to understand death by an analogy, but by an analogy which is in no sense arbitrarily chosen. Thus *Stirb und werde*, (Die and become) is shown to be a fact of experience and death can only be the paradoxical culmination of this inner struggle of existence.

"*Wer nicht von Grund aus todt ist, der weiss nicht das Geringste von der Heiligkeit, die Gott seinen lieben Freunden je offenbarte*". [68] (He who is not dead from the ground up knows absolutely nothing of the holiness which God has always revealed to his dear friends.)

We others, who have had no similar experience of our destiny, try simply to understand, and as men and philosophers — we also move towards life. "*O monstrum vitæ et mortis profunditas.*" (How monstrous is life and how profound is death)

THE MORAL PROBLEM
OF SUICIDE

"There is nothing in the world to which
a man has a more unassailable title
than to his own life and person"

A. SCHOPENHAUER

Paul Louis
Landsberg

PARIS, 1937

The Moral Problem
of Suicide

I TRADITIONAL ARGUMENTS [69]

I SHALL be told that the problem I propose to discuss simply does not exist, or, at any rate, does not
exist for Christians. We all know that Christianity,
and the Catholic Church in particular, and all moral
theologies, whether Catholic or Protestant, consider
suicide to be mortal sin, and do not admit that it can
be justified in any circumstances whatsoever. All this
is quite clear, and there seems to be nothing more to
be said. Suicide is forbidden by divine authority and
that ought to be enough. It is indeed true that the
believer should accept such a pronouncement as
authentic and final, even when he is not capable of
grasping the reasons on which it is founded. There is
such a thing as implicit obedience, just as there is an
implicit faith. This obedience is not blind ; it is based,
like faith, both on evidence and upon spontaneous
acceptance. However, this evidence is not the particular content of such and such an article of faith, or
such and such a moral precept, but the fundamental
evidence and the spontaneous acceptance of the
intrinsic goodness and justice of the authority which
reveals, teaches, orders and forbids. So far, all is
straightforward.

But no one will deny that we have the right and even, in a certain sense, the duty to try to understand more clearly what we believe, and to seek for the reasons for the rules we should obey. This is St. Anselm's *fides quaerens intellectum*. And I should like to add that, in my case, there seem to be two particular reasons which do indeed make the question of suicide a very real problem, which neither Christian philosophy nor theology has the right to overlook :

1. I have been profoundly impressed by the fact that, of all existing moralities, Christian morality is, strictly speaking, the only one to forbid suicide outright, without being willing to allow any exceptions. There are, it is true, some philosophers, particularly Plato and the Platonists, who cherish a certain aversion to suicide. But we have no example of a non-Christian philosopher who considers it to be in every case a grave sin or crime. We do, it is true, find in the ethics of certain communities a marked disapproval of suicide, for instance, among the Jews of the Old Testament, the Buddhists, and the followers of the orphic mysteries ; but here also we find a considerable number of exceptions which are considered to be justified, and there is no question of an intransigent principle. The sacred horror of suicide is a peculiarly and exclusively Christian phenomenon.

2. From the philosophic angle, there is always a moral problem wherever there is a temptation latent in human nature itself. It should be enough to point out that cases of suicide have occurred at all times

68

and amongst all peoples - and even amongst the so-called "primitives", to a much greater extent than is generally admitted - to show that it is a temptation of fairly common occurrence.

And further, the very way in which the Christian religion opposes suicide by stigmatising it as an extreme aberration, presumes the existence of such a temptation. But above all, we need only to have lived and to have understood only a little of the human heart, to know that man can welcome the idea of death. It is not true that man always loves life unconditionally. Such is human suffering that any psychic life that is at all developed will necessarily be subject to this temptation or at least know moments when man will wish for death. And as soon as there is temptation we have to protect ourselves, and this self-protection must have a positive meaning which can even serve to make our morality deeper and more conscious. The great temptations are active forces which are necessary to the moral evolution of an extremely imperfect creature that is nevertheless destined to perfection, that is to say, to man. It is not sufficient to point purely and simply to a divine command when humanity is challenged by one of its specific and, so to say, basic temptations. Man has to respond with his whole being, with the full weight of his existence, in action, in feeling and also in his intellect. All serious moral philosophy is the theoretical expression of the outcome of such a struggle against temptations latent in the human condition itself.

In view of this, perhaps I shall be allowed to affirm the existence of an authentic problem and of the philosopher's right to discuss it, although it may be objected that all has already been said. So let us first of all follow, *grosso modo*, the principal arguments brought forward in all discussion of the problem.

SINCE suicide is a fact of familiar, daily occurrence - as the columns of the press bear witness - there is, first of all, a vast, diffused discussion of the subject amongst the public, which does deserve a moment's consideration. Here we frequently find an argument against suicide, which is commonly put forward by the unintelligent. It is very customary to find all suicides condemned as cowards. This is a typically bourgeois argument which I find ridiculous. How can we describe as cowardly the way of dying chosen by Cato or Hannibal, Brutus or Mithridates, Seneca or Napoleon ? There are certainly far more people who do not kill themselves because they are too cowardly to do so, than those who kill themselves out of cowardice. The argument can only be valid on an entirely different level. It may be that compared wich the *supernatural* courage of Christ and the saints, even the courage of Cato might appear a form of cowardice. But on an ordinary human level it is more frequently the courageous who, in certain circumstances, decide to kill themselves. Montaigne said of Cato : "This was a man chosen by nature to show the heights which can be attained by human steadfastness and constancy . . . Such courage is above philosophy." It was the warlike, courageous nations -

such as Sparta, Rome, Japan in its best periods - that considered suicide not only permissible but, in a number of cases, imperative. It is the pagan hero who prefers death, for instance, to the dishonour of defeat. It is the heroic nation that despises those who cling to life, whatever it may be and at whatever cost. The evidence of Plutarch seems infinitely more correct and more convincing than the opinions of a bourgeois materialism. The Christian religion, which condemns suicide as sin, considers it far more the sin of Lucifer than a banal cowardice. And further, nothing is more opposed to the spirit of Christianity than to treat the prolongation of empirical existence as an absolute value, or even as a value of a very high order. Similarly, there is no weight in the argument that suicide is always proof of a weakness of will. There is a will to live and a will to die, and the latter has to be extremely powerful before it leads to a real suicide.

And then there are those, on the other hand, who still support the right to a voluntary choice of death by countering the Christian argument as follows : You say that voluntary death is contrary to the will of God who created us. But if this is true, why then did God create us in such a way that we have the capacity and opportunity to kill ourselves ? - This argument is all too easy to refute, but it is perhaps more important to learn from it. The fallacy of course is obvious. Every crime and sin is in a sense possible to man and the same argument could be used to justify murder and robbery. The whole significance of a moral prohibition is that it is there to guide a man who has

71

the capacity to act otherwise. But in the case of suicide we must dwell for a moment on the importance of the fact that man is a being who can kill himself and may not do so. This is quite different from being incapable of doing so. Temptation is an experience of the difference between the vertigo of power and the decision of duty. The manifold possibilities open to the unstable, intelligent, imperfect creatures that we are, form the basis of all moral problems. A genuine moral problem is always the immense problem of man taken from a given angle. There are few facts so profoundly characteristic of the abyss of liberty and the power of reflection by which man makes himself, up to a certain point, master of his actions and even of his existence. This is precisely why man lives out his moral problems, and he has therefore to live this problem of self-inflicted death. The temptation to suicide is part of the vertigo of his dangerous liberty. If, therefore, the fact of being able to kill oneself is not a justification for suicide, it is nevertheless the basis of a specifically human problem. For the temptation to fathom the full extent of his freedom is one of the profoundest temptations known to man. I may remind you of Dostoievsky's Kirilov, the man who wishes to kill himself in order to become free, or rather to prove the absolute freedom of man, man's divinity and the measure of what is possible to man. Dostoievsky, who knew better than any other the terrible nature of human freedom, has, in this fictional character, given the clearest possible expression to the fundamental motive underlying the temptation to suicide.

It is therefore not surprising that philosophic discussion of the problem has always centred on the
problem of liberty. I have no room to do justice to the
quality of this discussion. It is no exaggeration to say
that the problem of the free choice of death is one of
the most fundamental problems of all the great moral
philosophies. All I can do here is to review briefly the
stoic point of view, which is particularly important and
well-developed. Stoicism, particularly after Panetius,
that is to say, after he had assimilated the virtues of
the Roman character, was essentially a philosophy
of freedom, or rather, of liberation. The Epicureans
and the first Greek Stoics treated the question of a
choice of death with calm. The metaphor most frequently employed was that to kill oneself was just like
leaving the theatre when one was bored or did not
like the play. Such was more or less the attitude
adopted by Petronius, so glorified by Tacitus. Saint-
Evrémond died in the same manner, with a smile of
disillusionment on his lips. The early Stoa and Epicurus considered that death was no concern of ours ;
so long as we exist, death does not ; when death
exists, we do not. This doctrine became much more
dynamic with Seneca and all those who followed his
doctrine and his example, which Tacitus, the great
martyrographer of the stoic suicide, ascribes to the
dominance of reason. Reason tells us that we must
make ourselves independent of anything that happens to us outside our own will and choice. Therefore
the most essential quality is to be able to despise
such things as do happen to us independently of our
own will, and above all, to despise death. Stoic wis-

dom did not necessarily entail death, but it depended on a frame of mind in which the whole person has become the free arbiter of his own "living or dying" according to the dictates of reason. The Stoic was a man who could die if reason so ordained. The empirical capacity to die, which is common to all human beings, was transformed in the Stoic into a capacity which could function immediately if fate required it of reason. It is not the external act of suicide which is glorified, but rather the inner liberty which permits and insists on it, in certain cases. In such circumstances suicide is the *via libertatis*. Then the voice of Seneca says to man : "You should not live in necessity, since there is no necessity to live." It is Cato who will not survive if the Republic has lost its freedom, it is Hannibal who refuses to live as a prisoner of the Romans, it is Lucrece who will not survive the dishonour she has suffered. And in modern times, it is Condorcet who will not live to see the degradation of the Revolution. There are the countless heroes of Plutarch ; there is Chamfort saying good-bye to a world where the heart must break or grow cold — or the suicides after the German defeat in 1918, and more recently after the defeat of France. From the stoic viewpoint the death of Socrates is also voluntary, in the sense that he refuses to live as a fugitive far from the City. This strong-willed and rationalist Roman philosophy of the person *sui compos* - master of his own life - is the last great philosophy of Greco-Roman antiquity before the victory of Christianity. There is still an echo of it in Celsus, who follows Marcus Aurelius in reproaching the Christian martyrs. Not for their death, which he considers to be a choice of death, but for dying from a passionate fanaticism of love for a God whom Celsus considered an illusion, whereas, according to him, they should have died from a cold decision of the mind. Stoicism has never completely died out and the conflict between Christianity and the stoic morality has continued to disturb the conscience of Europe, particularly since the Renaissance. In any case, what is important here is that it is a philosophy of the autonomy of the reasonable being, the keystone of which is the philosophy of a free choice of death.

It is understandable that the struggle with Stoicism should have led the Christian Church to give explicit reasons for its condemnation of self-inflicted death. But I have not found, nor, I believe, has anyone else, any detailed discussion of the 'problem' from the Christian angle before St. Augustine. This has led M.A. Bayet to maintain, in his book - which is a source of much valuable information on the subject - that the condemnation of suicide is not authentically Christian, but something introduced into Christianity by St. Augustine, from a certain "slave morality" of antiquity. I believe, however, that the early Christians did not discuss the problem, simply because they considered it had been solved for them by the example of Christ and the martyrs. This is a point which we should discuss for a moment.

Bayet, like the Stoics, considers the Christian martyrs, or at least those martyrs who in fact offered themselves up to a violent death, as so many suicides. Whether he is right or wrong depends on one's definition of suicide. And the choice of definition is in itself an indication of the point of view from which the problem is to be discussed. The definition Bayet has chosen, which enables him to consider the actions of the martyrs as examples of suicide (the definition which underlies all his argument), is the one given by Durkheim in his sociological study of suicide : "Any case of death which results directly or indirectly from the positive or negative act of the victim who knew that it was bound to produce this result." This definition would in fact justify the contention that Christianity permitted suicide in the case of martyrs, a contention which seems to me to be justified neither from the Christian nor from the philosophical standpoint. Firstly, this very elaborate definition is still too narrow in that it does not cover the cases of unsuccessful attempts at suicide. Suicide is not just a type of death; it is a human act. In spite of Durkheim's famous instructions with regard to sociological method, we are not here dealing with "things", but with human acts. If the unsuccessful suicide was really inspired by serious intention, then he was a suicide. Naturally I am not speaking of those more or less hysterical attempts at suicide which are not true suicides even if they should accidentally result in death. I am thinking of the frequent attempts known to all doctors, which fail for purely technical reasons. These cases are often hushed up, but the majority of those who finally succeed in killing themselves have a past history of many previous attempts. The best known historical instance is that of Napoleon, which has been so well described by Caulaincourt. [70] I myself believe that such cases are extremely frequent. Further, if suicide were, in fact, merely a form of death and not a human act, public opinion and the law would be at fault in holding that self-inflicted death is not suicide in cases of unsound mind, since there is no responsibility. But Durkheim's definition is much too comprehensive, on the other hand, since it overlooks the essential difference between the act of not running away from death, and the act of killing oneself. The whole point of this distinction is that there are many who kill themselves in order to avoid a certain form of death. Hundreds and thousands of persons have killed themselves in this way, either in the prisons of the Inquisition - particularly of the Spanish Inquisition in order to escape being burnt - or during the French Revolution, like the Girondins and others, in order to avoid the ignominy of the guillotine. Neither is it unknown in our present century, in the prisons of the Tcheka and elsewhere. On the other hand, during the great persecutions, the Christian martyrs underwent the most hideous forms of death in the strength of a triumphant faith, without attempting to kill themselves beforehand. We must therefore categorically reject a definition which is superficial in spite of all its claims to objectivity, since it permits this confusion of two totally opposing attitudes. Bayet's argument that Christianity was not originally totally opposed to suicide rests solely on this fallacious definition.

It seems only fair, however, to put forward my own definition of suicide, which I believe to be simple and accurate : the act by which a human being deliberately creates what he considers to be an effective and adequate cause of his own death. The theorists who look at Christianity from outside may, in fact, be easily led astray by the almost total contempt for empirical existence displayed by the martyrs. This fact is important, since it demonstrates once again that Christianity has not been led to condemn suicide from any attachment to earthly life or from any particularly exalted view of its value. In the story of the martyrdom of St. Peter, for instance, we find a contempt for death and empirical existence which is inspired by Christ's example. "My brethren, my children, we must not flee suffering, for Christ's sake, since He Himself of His own free will, accepted death for our sake." This is also the significance of the legend of *Quo Vadis*. But this is far from justifying the fantastic idea which tries to make of Christ a type of suicide. To kill oneself to avoid the Cross and to suffer martyrdom on the Cross are not exactly the same thing. We should be quite clear that nothing was further from the minds of the early Christians than to condemn a self-inflicted death in the name of any loyalty to our empirical existence. The contempt for earthly life amongst early Christians was so extreme that to modern eyes it might sometimes seem even monstrous. Take, as an example, a passage from the Epistle to the Romans of Ignatius the martyr; "Let me be fodder for the beasts. . . . I am the corn of God; I must be ground in the jaws of beasts. . . . I hope to meet wild beasts of a suitable disposition and, if necessary, I shall caress them, so that they may devour me immediately." Those who turn Christianity into a sort of virtuous optimism proper to all decent people, will never understand the attitude of true Christians to death, neither, as we shall see, will they understand the deeper reason underlying the Christian rejection of self-inflicted death. The magistrate who said to Dionysius the martyr, "It is good to live", received the reply, "Far other is the light we seek". Modern man is not superior, but definitely inferior to the Stoics. He has to be reminded that Christianity also condemns all forms of euthanasia, which must indeed be scandalous and hideously paradoxical to all but the heroic cast of mind.

But to return to St. Augustine, who was led to discuss the problem in his arguments with the Donatists (a Christian and belligerent sect which admitted suicide), and above all in his struggle with the Stoics. His admirable text, which is the foundation of all Christian philosophy on this subject, can be found in the first chapter of the *Civitas Dei*. You will remember the events which gave rise to the book : Rome, the Eternal City, The City, in short, the holy capital of civilisation and the Empire, had fallen for the first time in 410, to the barbarian invader. She had been partially destroyed and terribly ravaged by Alaric. The Bishop of Hippo, the apologist of the Church, wrote his great work in order to prove that Christianity was not the cause of this shattering event, and that the fall of Rome was far from implying the fall of the religion which, since Constantine, had been to some extent the Roman religion. So he was compelled to tackle the stoic philosophy from the Christian point of view, since Stoicism had remained to a large degree

the philosophy of the Roman nobility, and was apparently being used as the philosophical basis of the
argument that Christianity and its slave morality had
been responsible for the decadence of Rome. Christian women were, in particular, reproached for not
having killed themselves rather than fall into the
hands of the barbarians, which inevitably implied the
loss of their virginity. St. Augustine replies first of all
that the essence of virginity is not a physical state but
a moral fact. It can be lost morally without being lost
physically but, what is still more important, when a
woman loses her physical virginity without any con-
sent of the will, as in the case or the women raped
during the sack of Rome, she does not lose her
moral virginity; she is innocent and not dishonoured
and therefore has no reason to kill herself.

When discussing the classic instance of Lucrece,
St. Augustine insists on the spiritual morality of Christians. But in the main he counters the stoic argument
with the assertion that suicide is always and every-
where a crime. The arguments that he uses reappear
again and again in Christian literature down to our
own days. The principal argument is as follows; to kill
oneself is to kill a man, therefore suicide is homicide.
Homicide is inexcusable and is forbidden in the Ten
Commandments. With all respect, I hardly feel that
the argument is adequate. The commandment cannot and should not be interpreted to cover every act
which involves as its deliberate consequence the
death of a man. The Christian tradition, apart from a
few sects, has always allowed two important exceptions : war and capital punishment. St. Augustine

knows this very well, and therefore he treads warily. Thus he says : "*Ubique si non licet privata potestate hominem occidere vel nocentem, cujus occidendi licentiam lex nulla concedit; profecto etiam qui se ipsum occidet, homicida est.*" The stress is put on *privata potestate* and on cases where there is no legal sanction. But the moment we begin to make moral distinctions between the different types of cases which may involve the death of a man, one may just as well make a distinction between suicide and the murder of someone else. In my opinion, it is even necessary to do so. In the first place, if we are deciding something which affects our own life, we are in a totally different position from deciding something which affects the life of another. What would be an act of violent hostility towards another cannot be the same towards ourselves, if it is we who decide on the act. In many cases, the man who kills himself has no intention of destroying his person, but rather of saving it. Rarely, if ever, does he aim at annihilation. There is a smack of sophistry about this moral identification of the two acts when their dissimilarity is so striking. As for the commandment, we must not make it say what it does not say. It is universally accepted that it does not forbid a just war or the death penalty, but it is difficult to maintain that it does condemn suicide, at any rate unconditionally. The Old Testament records as many suicides as it does wars, and some of them are glorified, as in the cases of Samson and Saul. Christians have made out, in the case of these biblical suicides, that a direct and exceptional command from God may hallow acts which are quite

81

immoral in themselves. This is the paradox taken up by Kierkegaard, of Abraham, who is prepared, in faith and obedience, to become the murderer of his son. It is Calvin's justification of political sedition when ordained by God. However, the Old Testament chronicles its suicides without insisting on any such supernatural justification. There is no reason for believing that the Decalogue was intended to cover cases of suicide. And the chain of reasoning which plays such a large part in Augustine's text, is certainly not an example of his profoundest thinking.

There is an allusion to Job which allows us to suspect that he has not spoken his whole mind. The reason is obvious. He was dealing with Romans. It often happens that the brilliant orator and advocate, the direct descendant of Cicero, gets the upper hand and then he speaks *ad extra* and *ad hominem*. Thus, in the middle of his expositions we find a beautiful passage which counters the famous example of Cato, so highly praised by his own master, Cicero, not with a Christian counterpart, but with the example of Regulus, who returned to Carthage in order to keep his word, in the certainty that he would be killed by the Carthaginians.

Unfortunately, I do not have the space to analyse Augustine's text as it deserves, nor to follow up in proper detail the evolution of Christian doctrine with regard to suicide. We find no substantial argument added to the reasoning of the Father of the Church in the period between St. Augustine and St. Thomas. But St. Thomas is not satisfied with St. Augustine's arguments and cries to substitute others.

The fresh arguments that he adduces are three :

1. Suicide is contrary to man's natural inclinations, contrary to natural law and contrary to charity — to that charity which a man owes to himself. *Amor bene ordinatus incipit a semet ipsum.* What then are we to make of this argument ? First of all, if suicide were, in every case, contrary to the natural law, it would not occur, or only in a very few exceptional or pathological cases. I must confess I find it difficult to see that something can be against natural law when it is practised, accepted and often honoured amongst all non-Christian peoples. Suicide is far from being contrary to human nature. The human animal's will to live is neither unlimited nor unconditional. It remains to be seen whether suicide must, in every case, be contrary to the love that we should have for ourselves. Suicide, no doubt, deprives us of that good which is life. But in fact, and from the Christian's point of view, this good is of highly dubious quality ; and, in any case, it is not the highest good and often rather more like an evil. To deprive oneself of a purely relative good to avoid an evil which is expected to be greater, such as the loss of honour or freedom, is not an act directed against oneself. And this is very often precisely the case of the man who kills himself. It would be much more reasonable to say that he kills himself out of too great a self-love. Consider also the importance of the almost ontological concept of war in the ancient world and Proteus's suicide out of friendship. If we interpret it on a deeper level, then the argument runs : he who kills himself deprives himself of salvation, which would be the total negation of that charity towards oneself required by the Gospels. But in this case we are arguing in circles, since we have an argument which sets out to prove that suicide is a sin, by assuming the premise that suicide is already mortal sin. In fact, the vast majority of those who kill themselves have no desire or intention of forfeiting their salvation. On the contrary, they say, like Doña Sol to Hernani : "Soon we shall be moving towards fresh light, together we shall spread our wings and fly with measured beat towards a better world." The case of Kleist and his woman friend is there to demonstrate the romantic suicide is not a purely lite- rary invention. Man finds, on the other side of the grave, an imaginary home for the hopes which have been disappointed in life. There Werther will meet Lotte once more. "Death, tomb," he says, "What do such words mean?" In the majority of cases, the one who kills himself seeks neither perdition nor extinc- tion ; the life he knows seems far less desirable than something which is vague and unknown, but at any rate something. The theological sin of despair is not defined as to the loss of such and such an empirical expectation, but as the loss of that fundamental hope in God and His Goodness which is the very life of the human heart. The loss of expectation is even a ne- cessary step in the Spiritual journey of the masters. It is therefore false to claim that all suicides are men without hope, in the theological sense. Personally, I go so far as to believe that man never despairs com- pletely, that it is impossible for him and contrary to his essential being, to despair. *Desesperare*, says St.

Thomas, *non est descendere in infernum*. He does not speak of suicide in his tremendous chapter on the sin of despair. In my view, despair is not a characteristic of man on earth, but perhaps only of Hell and the Devil. We do not even know what it is. The act of suicide does not, to me, express despair, but rather a wild and misguided hope directed to the vast unknown kingdom on the other side of death, I would even venture upon the paradox : men often kill themselves because they cannot and will not despair. This is why the idea of Hell, which fills the place of the unknown beyond, is such a strong 'disincentive' to suicide. Even Shakespeare, speaking with the voice of Hamlet, is held back by this dread of the terror of a future existence.

2. St. Thomas repeats the argument used by the platonic school, and particularly Aristotle, to discountenance suicide. Plato was, in fact, to some degree opposed to the idea of suicide : for reasons not unrelated to the enormous influence of the orphic mysteries on the spirit of his philosophy, and also because of his profound attachment to the idea of the *Polis* ; one has only to read Diogenes Laërtius to appreciate that suicide was almost the normal end of all Greek philosophers from Empedocles down to the Hellenistic period. But Plato gives the philosophers a place in the City and advises them not to desert this place. Aristotle turns it into the argument that a man belongs to his country and to society, and has no right to deprive them of his presence and activity by suicide. St. Thomas takes up this argument which would, perhaps, have a certain value in an ideal society ; but, in reality, people do often kill themselves because the very imperfect societies in which they are condemned to live prevent them from leading any form of creative life. So long as societies breed more forms of moral and material misery than need be our lot, it would be highly imprudent to authorise them to condemn those who try to escape from their authority by death. Man did not ask to be born into a society and he does not see why he should not be allowed to leave it by the best door left open, if life in such a society has lost all meaning for him. The argument may be valid in certain instances, where someone may in fact be abandoning an important social duty, but it is clearly inadequate as a general argument against suicide as such. Moreover, the same collectivist premise might lead to the opposite conclusion if an individual could no longer find a social justification for his existence. I would add that, to me, the argument seems inspired by a collectivist outlook, by the atmosphere of the Greek City which is essentially non-Christian. It is purely and simply anti-personalist to try to decide such an intimately personal question as to whether or not I have the right to kill myself, by reference to society. Suppose I die a little sooner or a little later, what has that to do with a society to which, in any case, I belong for so short a space ? Saint Thomas is taking up one of Aristotle's arguments, as he frequently does, without allowing for the profoundly non-Christian outlook which inspires his thinking both in detail and in the whole. The weakness of the social argument can be seen even more clearly in Kant. According to Kant, the man who feels tempted to commit suicide should consider whether the principle on which his decision is based could become a principle of general legislation. But man knows very well that he is faced every time with a particular situation, and that he is, as a person, unique. In modern Christian moralists the argument reappears in the form that man has no right to kill himself since this would constitute a crime against his family. But as a general argument, this also fails to convince. First of all, a lot of people have no families, or a shattered or detestable family, and secondly, the question is really far too personal to be decided by such arguments. Everyone dies sooner or later, and society and the family get over It. It is true that those who have a normal family life seldom kill themselves, like those who might happen to live in an ideal society. But all the same, the fact that there are so many suicides proves that many people do not find in their homes what they should find there. One of the most frequent types of suicide is the result of a love affair, often in the form of a suicide pact. It would be ridiculous to try to say to these unhappy creatures that they are proposing to commit a mortal sin because they are neglecting their duty towards their family. Why does no one say the same thing to the young people who go into monasteries, often against the wishes of the family ? This is another of those arguments — not St. Thomas's argument, but that of one's duty to the family — which reek of complacency. Suicide is often taken to be an act indicative of decadent and anarchistic individualism, overlooking the fact that amongst entirely healthy and even extremely warlike communities it is often considered, in certain circumstances, a social duty. But death is above all so much a personal and individual thing that the problems it creates transcend the social life of this planet.

3. By far the most weighty of St. Thomas's arguments is the third : We are God's property, just as the slave is the property of his master. Man is not *sui juris*. It is for God to decide on our life or death.

Leaving aside the comparison with the slave, which invites the stoic reply that it is precisely the free man who can kill himself, there is undoubtedly something strong and cogent in this argument. Suicide may be due to pride. Man can now prove that he can be *sicut Deus*. Montaigne has replied in defence of the stoic point of view : "God has given his leave enough when He puts us in such a state that living is worse than dying." The Thomist argument loses much of its value unless it is taken in a specifically Christian sense. If we were dealing with a God who was a tyrant and slave owner, the argument would clearly not suffice.

II A PERSONAL VIEW

I HAVE discussed certain traditional arguments, not really so much for their historic importance as to bring out the enormous complexity and difficulty of the problem. I turned hopefully to the early Christian Fathers for an answer to the question and, in fact, failed to find a really satisfactory reply. I might add that this seldom happens. Neither have I criticised for the pleasure of criticising such and such an argument, but for a much more serious reason. "We can only discuss something honourably in so far as we sympathise with it", says Goethe in *Werther* on the very topic of suicide. Picture to yourself a man who is very much tempted to suicide. Perhaps he has lost his family, or he despairs of the society in which he has to live, or maybe bitter suffering is depriving him of all grounds for hope. His present life is terrible, his future dark and menacing. Suppose you tell him he must live in order to obey the commandment, or in order not to sin against the love of oneself, or to do his duty to society and family, or finally, in order not to decide something himself that only God is entitled to decide : do you think you would convince this man in his misery and suffering ?

Of course you would not. He would find your arguments either suspicious or laughable. He might be restrained from suicide by technical difficulties, by cowardice or weakness of will, by a certain instinct for life or, as often happens, by an implicit faith in divine protection or by the fear of Hell. But these traditional arguments will probably be ineffective. So what he needs is not so much abstract arguments as an example. And here, I believe, we have in very truth the most magnificent and valuable example. It is the example of Christ. Here we must turn, not to the letter of the Old but to the spirit of the New Testament. To understand why Christianity is opposed to suicide, we must recall the fundamental character of Christian life which is, in all its forms, an attempt at the Imitation of Jesus Christ.

This effort implies a radical conversion of natural human attitudes, more especially with regard to suffering. The human being has, by nature, a horror of suffering and a desire for happiness. The man who kills himself almost always does so to escape from the suffering of this life towards an unknown happiness and calm. In any case he says in his heart, "I want to go somewhere else. I do not wish to endure this suffering which has no meaning and is beyond my strength".

It is here that the spirit of Christianity intervenes with its tremendous paradox. Yes, live and suffer. You should not be surprised that you suffer. If happiness were the meaning of life, it would indeed be a revolting and finally improbable condition. But the situation is different if life is a justification, the progress towards a transcendent goal, and if its meaning were in fact evident in suffering and achieved through suffering. "Lord, to suffer or to die", prays St. Theresa. Yes, in spite of all those optimistic believers, life is the carrying of a cross. But even the cross has a sacred meaning.

My belief is, therefore, that far from being one of the so-called natural laws, or the law of some peculiar common sense, the total prohibition of suicide can only be justified or even understood in relation to the scandal and the paradox of the Cross. It is true that we belong to God, as Christ belonged to God. It is true that we should subordinate our will to His, as Christ did. It is true that we should leave the decision as to our life or death to Him. If we wish to die, we have indeed the right to pray to God to let us die. Yet we must always add : Thy will, not mine, be done. But this God is not our master as if we were slaves. He is our Father. He is the Christian God who loves us with infinite love and infinite wisdom. If He makes us suffer, it is for our salvation and purification. We must recall the spirit in which Christ suffered the most horrible death. In certain circumstances, to refuse suicide is far from natural. To prefer martyrdom to suicide is a paradox peculiar to the Christian. It was precisely this element in the martyr's attitude which so very profoundly shocked the pagan philosophers. The martyrs refused suicide, not through a cowardly attachment to life, but because they found a strange happiness in following the example of Christ, and suffering for Him and with Him. It has been quite reasonably maintained that the fact that people are willing to die for a cause argues nothing as to the value of that cause. It is true that a great many persons have died for causes which we find deplorable. So it is in a different sense that the martyrs bear witness to Christianity. They do not prove any given theorerical truth, but they prove by their example that it is possible to live and die in a Christian manner. It is not their death, but their manner of dying which is important. They are witness in a very special way to the fact that Grace may enable a man to follow Christ in His attitude towards suffering and death, which is itself very far from natural. Their blessedness in, and to some extent through, suffering, far exceeds the somewhat frigid heroism of the ancient world. The vast majority of humanity is morally inferior to the Stoics. The Christian martyr is superior. The stoic virtue is quite probably the highest morality known to man outside the sphere of Christian Grace. The hero, master of his own death, stands above the mass of poltroons and slaves. "This noble despair, so worthy of the Romans", wrote Corneille. The saint is, as it were, a super-hero of specifically Christian character. It is his life that in fact demonstrates the argument. He shows that it is possible for man to live out his suffering by discovering a transcendental significance in its very depths. One cannot stress too strongly the paradoxical quality of all this, just as Kierkegaard has so rightly insisted on the paradoxical nature of the whole of Christianity. In order to gauge the paradox, we should remember what suffering is. The word is quickly said, but the subject itself is so vast, an authentic mystery. Even physical suffering can take on horrible forms. We are told that it will be limited and that consciousness, the precondition of suffering, fails at a certain level of pain. Perhaps : we know little about it. Man is always mistaken when he thinks he has reached the ultimate limit of human suffering. There are still the worst moral tortures. One falls, one falls from abyss to abyss. In periods like our own, one must feel frightened at the immensity of present human suffering. When one reads history, one is overwhelmed by what men have always and everywhere endured. Sickness, death, misery and all manner of peril, surround the human being. The optimists are having a joke at our expense. It is no exaggeration to speak, as Schopenhauer does, of a *ruchloser optimisimus*, a frivolous and criminal optimism.

The same judgment applies equally to those who immediately try to console you with talk of divine Providence and goodness. There is nothing more paradoxical than this divine love which chastens with fire and which has, according to Dante, created Hell. Even Providence is another paradox. All that is left is the example of Christ and of those men who were able to follow his example, showing that to do so they needed not to be gods, but only to be granted divine Grace, which is equally promised to us.

All that we can say to the suffering man who is tempted to commit suicide, is this : "Remember the sufferings of Christ and the martyrs. You must carry your cross, as they did. You will not cease to suffer, but the cross of suffering itself will grow sweet by virtue of an unknown strength proceeding from the heart of divine love. You must not kill yourself, because you must not throw away your cross. You need it. And enquire of your conscience if you are really innocent. You will find that if you are perhaps innocent of one thing for which the world reproaches you, you are guilty in a thousand other ways. You are a sinner. If Christ, who was innocent, suffered for others and, as Pascal said, has also shed a drop of blood for you, how shall you, a sinner, be entitled to refuse suffering? Perhaps it is a form of punishment. But divine punishment has this specific and incomparable quality, that it is not a revenge and that its very nature is purification. Whoever revolts against it, revolts in fact against the inner meaning of his own life."

There is no doubt that there is no justice here below. Criminal monsters carry all before them, and none suffers more than the saint. Here we approach the mystery of sin, which is so closely linked with this other mystery that the Christian finds the meaning of life in and through suffering. Man, we said, was a creature who could kill himself and should not do so. The meaning of this assertion now becomes clearer. The temptation exists, and there is rejection of this temptation. Where this rejection is authentically Christian, it is in the form of an act of love towards God, and towards suffering, not as suffering, which is impossible — algophilia is pathological, and even Christ faltered before His last agony, and prayed that it should be taken from Him — but towards suffering in so far as it contains a remedy desired by God.

Just as there is a qualitative difference between bourgeois and heroic morality, there is an abyss between natural morality on the one hand and the supernatural morality of Christianity on the other. Our reflections on the problem of suicide show this, just as any profound reflection on any moral problem of practical and vital importance must show it. Christianity is a new message. The truth of Stoicism lies in its understanding of the close relationship between human freedom and a contempt for death. Whoever is a slave to death is in fact also a slave to all the accidents of life. There is no liberation of the person unless the supreme and universal necessity of this mortal accident is transformed into a free act. But whereas Stoicism tries to acquire this freedom through the knowledge of the possibility of suicide, the Christian must acquire it through a loving accept-ance of the will of God. He may prefer life to death, or death to life according to the circumstances, but he must place the will of God with absolute sincerity before his own. Death is often a boon, and Swift was right to speak of "the dreadful aspect of never dying", but it is God who must set a term to our suffering.

There are other doctrines besides Christianity, which have given a positive, metaphysical signifi-cance to earthly suffering. The orphic mysteries - often considered as an early prototype of Christianity - saw suffering as a way to the liberation from the body. There is Buddhism, and the almost Buddhist philosophy of Schopenhauer. It is significant that these doctrines should be equally inimical to suicide. But there is nothing in these attitudes to compare with the Christian drama. To authentic Buddhism, as to Schopenhauer, suicide is an error, or a sort of *impasse*. What Buddha calls *thirst*, and Schopen-hauer, the *will to live*, cannot be overcome by suicide. Nor can one escape from existence by such violent means. The suicide is transformed, according to his *Karma*, but he does not attain *Nirvana*. We have seen, in fact, and I know it to be true in many cases I have known of personally, that the purpose of suicide was not the idea of extinction but of attaining an existence radically different from the one left behind by death. The Buddist's aversion to suicide is naturally not in any way comparable to the Christian rejection. In the first place, genuine Buddhism is far too intellectualised to entertain any general concept of sin. If anyone commits the error of refusing, by such an act of violence, to accept his suffering, he will suffer the consequence according to his *Karma*, and he will learn. That is all. Finally, and here the comparison may help us to establish a very important point, the moment of physical death has not the same quality of metaphysical decision for the Oriental as for the Christian. The stress placed by Christianity on this prohibition of suicide is no doubt partly explained by the idea that everything to do with death has a metaphysical aspect, an idea which is absolutely foreign to the East. What is horrible about suicide to the Christian is that there is little or no time left for repentance after the sin has been committed. In principle, therefore, canon law refuses Christian burial to the suicide, because he died within a state of mortal sin. There are, however, two exceptions : one, if the act is committed in a state or even a moment of mental unbalance, which excludes responsibility ; the other, if the suicide can be given the benefit of any doubt ; if, for instance, there is any possibility that he may have made an act of repentance. The existence of these two exceptions, and the obvious difficulty of excluding them completely in any particular case, have led the Church, particularly in modern times, to exercise indulgence. Principles cannot be changed, but there are more scruples about the mental health of the suicide, and a reluctance to assert that no act of repentance, which might be something like a lightning flash of conscience, could have taken place. Thus judgment is left to God, that is to say judgment on the person, not judgment on the principle of the act itself.

Before drawing to a close, I should briefly mention one argument against the Christian point of view. If suffering is sacred and contains the meaning of life, why are we entitled to struggle against it? If we have this right, and even this duty, why should we not have the right to withdraw from suffering by suicide if there is no other way out? I agree at once that man has the right to struggle against the miseries of existence. The contrary would obviously lead to moral absurdities, such as the immorality of medicine. But we should not overestimate the struggle, neither in its importance nor in its chances of success. It is natural and laudable for man to struggle against sickness, cruelty, misery and the rest. But in point of fact there has been no progress in human happiness in all our history, but rather the reverse. Everything we know leads us to believe that the so-called primitive peoples are much happier than we are. What is false is not the struggle against suffering, but the illusion that we can destroy it. The means of fighting this suffering is, above all, work, which was given to man both as punishment and cure. But this effort to combat suffering cannot be compared with the act of suicide. Suicide is something on its own. It seems to me to be a flight by which man hopes to recover Paradise Lost instead of trying to deserve Heaven. The desire for death which is unleashed when temptation becomes our master is, psychologically speaking, the desire to regress to a pre-natal state. To vanish, to get away from it all. Stekel and others have given us a precise psychological analysis of suicide, the longing for the abyss, the mother, the return. The whole process could be described in Freudian terms. Theologically speaking, there is, in fact, the vague illusion of a return to Paradise. The Rousseau-Werther type of suicide is usually conscious of this obscure motivation. In this connection one could quote many interesting passages from Goethe, Senancourt, Amiel, and others. But Christ guides us through struggle and suffering towards a brighter light. The god, or rather, goddess, of suicide thrusts us back upon the mother's breast. In this sense, suicide is an infantilism. It is this quality of regression which prevents any comparison between suicide and man's normal struggle against suffering. It is the failure of all other means which, in the majority of cases, leads to suicide; it is the universal experience of powerlessness. This convergence of one disaster after the other, destroying all possibility of living and struggling, is the common factor in the biographies of all suicides. Without going into the details of some personal biographies I have myself studied, let me remind you of two great classics : *Werther* and *Anna Karenina*. You can see in these two books how life and his own

character combined form a trap for man. And it is precisely what is most noble in man that may urge him
to suicide. If you can imagine a Werther or an Anna
Karenina who were both slightly more frivolous, you
will see that their problems might have been solved.
But you will see also that in such cases the only truly
positive and honourable solution would be that complete conversion required by Christ.

It is entirely clear that the Christian apologists were
well aware of this real and profound explanation of
the Christian attitude to suicide. Saints such as
Augustine and Thomas Aquinas were certainly far
better aware of it than I. Why then did they not give
it? I think largely because such things were taken for
granted in that period of militant and heroic Christianity. Do not forget that St. Augustine only mentions
this problem when he is addressing Roman pagans,
in defence against the charge that Christianity had
grown weaker. Nowadays, when it has frequently
become painfully mediocre, it is again attacked by a
new and fanatical paganism, which also has its
moments of heroism. Either Christianity will disappear, or it will recover its original virtues. We do not
believe that it can disappear, but it must certainly
renew itself by becoming aware of its true nature. It
is therefore useful, by dwelling on one specific problem, to show that Christian morality is not some sort
of natural, reasonable and universal morality, with
perhaps a little more sensation in it than some others, but the manifestation in life of a paradoxical revelation. It cannot be superfluous either, to remind
oneself today that Christian morality is not a morality

of compromise, but that it requires heroism more profound, more absurd and, in a way, more intransigent,
than any other. In other words, we have become
explicitly conscious of things which, in an age still
close to martyrs, could be taken for granted.

ANNOTATIONS

1 *Dictionnaire Philosophique*, Vol.14, p.63.

2 Voltaire uses the words "its experience" and not "experience". This use of the pronoun shows that he is speaking of the common experience of humanity, an experience enlarged by science ; this implies a quantitative concept of experience. Thus an empirical interpretation seems unavoidable both from the philological and philosophic angle. Voltaire adds (*loc. cit.*), "A child brought up alone and transported to a desert island would have no more idea of death than a cat or a plant."

3 Max Scheler, "Tod und Fortleben" in *Schriften aus dem Nachlass*, Vol.I. Berlin, 1933.

4 Huizinga, *Le Déclin du Moyen Age*, Chap.II, La vision de la Mort. Paris, 1932.

5 See Frazer. (*The Fear of the Dead*. The Binjwar believe . . . that only evildoers survive harmful spirits.) According to Huizinga (*loc. cit.*), death and the dead man are identified in the mediæval Dances of Death.

6 I Corinthians XV, 55-57. It was one of the factors in the tragedy of Nietzsche that he saw Christianity through the eyes of Schopenhauer.

7 Heidegger's enquiries go almost immediately beyond the experience of the death of another and follow a course entirely different from my own. See *Sein und Zeit*, Vol 1. Halle, 1927.

8 Georges Duhamel, poet and doctor, has given an incomparable description of this sympathy in *l'Humaniste et l'automate*. Paris, 1934.

9 François Mauriac, *Journal*, Paris, 1935, p.53. "In the frightening confusion of feeling which we experience at the sight of death, there is also a sense of being cheated ; he whom we love is there and is no longer there."

10 Mauriac, *loc. cit.* "For a corpse is essentially an absence, something left behind, rejected, in fact, the remains."

11 This is the "everyman" in Baudelaire's saying : "God is the eternal confidant in this tragedy of which everyman is hero." (*Mon cœur mis à nu*).

12 It should be remembered that this "everyman" is the exact opposite of the "one" who is always a public creature. Montaigne seems to have been the first to state the identity of anthropological and individual generality in his well-known chapter "On Repentance" : "Everyman carries in himself the whole nature of the human condition." But the highest form of this symbolic and real identity is surely found in the Gospel of the Son of Man.

13 Paul Voivenel, author of a book of deep wisdom and experience, *Le médecin devant la douleur et la mort*. Paris, 1934.

14 The act of dying, which is always unique, may also be the most personal as Rilke has shown in the unforgettable pages of *Die Aufzeichnungen des Malte Laurids Brigge*. Leipzig, 1920.

15 Heidegger does not seem to grasp the importance of this distinction. His "*Mitsein*" is always a highly formalised concept. His philosophy does not include love, just as it includes neither faith nor hope. Jaspers with his idea of "communication" comes much closer to the possibility we are discussing. Cf. Jaspers, *Philosophie*, Vol.II.

16 If religion, for instance, offers us concrete pictures of the torments suffered by souls or even bodies in purgatory or hell, the situation is changed and pity becomes possible.

17 Miguel de Unamuno, *Avant et après la Révolution*. Paris, 1933, p.178.

18 Cf. my book *Einleitung in die philosophische Anthropologie*. Frankfurt, 1934, and my essay "La conception de la personne", *Esprit*, No.27, 1934.

19 In certain thinkers the pleasurable quality of anguish has a quality of nihilism.

20 Hebrews, XI, 2.

21 *Vida de Don Quixote y de Sancho*, 1905. Chap.
XLIV 1935. M. de Unamuno expresses this conviction, of which he rarely speaks, at the end of the mystical sonnet, *La Sima*. "Life, our true life, life, this
hope that immolates itself and lives thus, in immola-
tion, waiting."

22 V.A.Sternberger, *Der verstandene Tod*. Eine
Untersuchung über Martin Heidegger's Existenzial-
ontologie. Leipzig, 1934, pp. 83, 131, 143. This book
makes a fundamental criticism of Heidegger's nihilism which is very necessary to destroy its attraction.

23 [Landsberg makes a fundamental distinction
between *espérance*, the spiritual virtue, and *espoir* to
which he ascribes a purely temporal significance.
Both would normally be translated by hope in the
English language. To avoid confusion, in spite of the
fact that *espérance* might also mean expectation, I
have translated *espérance* as hope and *espoir* as
expectation.] (*Translator's Note*).

24 Paul Valéry has expressed this admirably in
Variété, Paris, 1926, in *The Crisis of the Spirit*. "But
expectation is only man's mistrust of the precise fore-
casts of his own mind. It suggests that any conclusion unfavourable to his being must be an error of the
mind." This passage has provoked the anger of
Unamuno's, as shown in his *Agonia del Christian-
ismo*, because it asserts a truth about expectation

without indicating that the contrary is true of hope.

25 Perhaps one might apply the word "hopeless-ness" (*désespoir*) to this general state of disillusion-ment with regard to temporal expectations. In Pascal the term *ennui* has often precisely this meaning. Cf. *Pensées* (Ed. Brunschvig, sect.II, 168 and 171, with commentary). In Kierkegaard it is not so much a question of hopelessness (*désespoir*) but of despair itself (*désespérance*). S, Kierkegaard, *Traité du dés-espoir*. N.R.F., 1932.

26 Epistle to the Romans, V, 5. The relationship be-tween the hope which is natural to man as person, as typified in Goethe's *Orphische Urworte*, and the supernatural hope which is provided by the revela-tion of Christ, seems to be somewhat similar to the analogy between immortality and resurrection. In both cases hope includes certainty, but these cer-tainties are of a different order. The hope of which I am speaking is therefore not the theologal virtue. I am describing the point in human nature whereby this virtue can and must enter, if the possibility of despair is to be finally overcome.

27 This category of *Everyman* corresponds in St. Augustine to the term *nos.* See, for instance, the last chapter of the Confessions : *et nos alio tempore moti sumus ad bene faciendum . . . priori autem tempore ad male faciendum movebamus*. The whole of this supremely important chapter is informed by his sense of the encounter and the contrast between man and God.

28 *The Confessions of St. Augustine*, Everyman Edition, p.56.

29 *Conf.,* IV, 4. "Quo dolore contenebratum est cor meum ; et quid quid aspiciebam mors erat. Et erat mihi patria supplicium, et paterna domus mira infelicitas ; et quidquid cum illo communicaveram, sine illo in cruciatum immanem verterat. Expetebant eum undique oculi mei, et non dabatur mihi ; et oderam omnia, quia non haberunt eum, nec jam mihi dicere poterant : 'Ecce veniet' sicut cum viveret quando absens erat. Factus eram ipse mihi magna quæstio et interrogabam animam meam quare tristis esset, et quare conturbaret me valde ; et nihil noverat respondere mihi. Et si dicebam 'Spera in Deum' juste non obtemperabat : quia verior erat et melior homo quem carissimum amiserat, quam phantasma in quod sperare jubebatur. Solus fletus erat dulcis mihi et successerat amico meo in delictis animi mei." The perpetual repetition of the "et" is the literary device by which St. Augustine expresses his *ennui*.

30 *Conf.,* IV, 6, "Mirabar enim cœteros mortales vivere, quia ille quem quasi non moriturum dilexeram, mottuus erat; et me magis, quia illi alter eram, vivere illo mortuo mirabar. Bene quidam dixit de amico suo : 'Dimidium animæ meæ'. Nam ego sensi animam meam et animam illius unam fuisse animam in duobus corporibus." On the death of the Grand Duchess Louise, Goethe said to Eckermann : "Der

Tod ist doch etwas so seltsames, daß man ihn, unerachtet aller Erfahrüng, bei einem uns teueren Gegenstände nicht für möglich hält, und er immer als etwas unglaubliches und unerwartetes auftritt." (Death, in fact, is so strange a thing that in spite of all experience we consider it impossible in the case of someone we love, and it always occurs like something unbelievable and unexpected.)

31 *Conf.,* V, 7. "Ego mihi remanseram infelix locus, ubi nec esse possem, nec inde recedere."

32 Cf. my book, *Wesen und Bedeutung der platonischen Akademie.* Bonn, 1923, particularly *Phaedo,* p. 64 et seq. We should not forget that this philosophy is a Mystery, a Greek Mystery in spiritual form.

33 One inevitably thinks of the spirits with whom mediums claim to communicate.

34 Isolation is, of course, the opposite of solitude, which may be a means to personal communion.

35 In the Mysteries, the Mother, Nature in the form of a goddess, seems to have been the immortal reality in which man participated through death and rebirth.

36 Diogenes Laërtius, X, 139.

37 Cicero, *Tuscul. Disp. I,* and *Cato Major,* 18-66.

38 Lucretius, III, 898. (M. Budé's text). "Nec videt in vera nullum fore morte alium se qui possit vivos sibi se lugere peremptum stansque jacentem." Thus the anguish of death lies in a fictitious duplication of the individual, and the annihilation of the individual should therefore annihilate any meaning which death might have for us. Cf. also Marcus Aurelius, *in se ipsum* : "The man that fears death fears either an absence of sensation or sensations of a different order. But if there is no more sensation, he will not feel any pain, and if he acquires sensations of a different order, he will be a living being of a different order, and will not cease to live."

39 Seneca, *Epist. ad Lucilium*, IV. "Nullum malum quod extremum est. Mors ad te venit ? Timenda erat, si tecum esse posset : necesse est aut non perveniat aut transeat." When Seneca was reproached for having borrowed a tenet from an alien sect, he replied with the famous remark : "Omne quod verum est, meum est." (Everything that is true, is mine.)

40 *Loc. cit.*, IV. "Ex quo natus es, duceris."

41 *Loc. cit.*, XXXVI. "Desinunt ista, non pereunt." Cf. also Marcus Aurelius, *loc. cit.*, II, 7. To him death is the dissolution of the living organism. See also Epictetus, *Encheiridion*, V.

42 *Loc. cit.*, XXX. "Tu autem mortem ut numquam timeas semper cogita.

43 *Loc. cit.*, LXXVII. "Fac tui juris quod alieni est." Cf. Epictetus, *loc. cit.*, XI. Death enters into the category of those things which should not concern us, since they are beyond our power to alter or select.

44 We must even change death into activity. "Non sit ipsa mors otiosa." Seneca, *De Otio*, VII,1.

45 This contempt for death should also extend to one's neighbour : "If you love your son or your wife, remember that you love human beings, and if they die, you will not suffer." Cf. Epictetus, *loc. cit.*, III.

46 *Loc. cit.*, LXXVIII. "Vita si moriendi virtus abest, servitus est."

47 *Loc. cit.*, XII. "Malum est in necessitate vivere ; sed in necessitate vivere, necessitas nulla est. Quidni nulla sit ? Patent undique ad libertatem viæ multæ, breves, faciles. Agamus deo gratias quod nemo in vita teneri potest."

48 The death of Socrates is a free death, in the stoic sense, although there is no question of suicide. Plato has already shown in *Phaedo*, 62, that the renunciation of flight has made this death one of free choice, not far removed from the philosophic suicide. For the stoic attitude towards the Christian martyrs, see P. de Labrielles *La réaction païenne*. Paris, 1934, pp.48, 78, 103. With regard to Seneca's socratic death, see Tacitus, *Annals*, XV, 62.

49 *Loc. cit.*, XXIV. "Mod de te pronunciatura est."

50 *The Story of My Death*. New York, Oxford University Press, 1933. Lauro de Bosis was a young poet who disappeared on a flight over Rome to scatter anti-fascist leaflets.

51 *Poner una banderilla* is a very frequent expression in Spain, meaning to make offensive remarks to someone.

52 *Matador* is derived from *matar*, to kill ; it means literally *the killer*.

53 Cf. Pascal, *Pensées*, III, 199 (Ed. Brunschvig, Vol. XIII, p.124). The Stoic, as we have seen, is the man without God, who neither can nor will despair entirely. His immobility both conceals and reveals his expectation. For the dialectical relationship between the Stoic and the bullfighter, see José Bergamin *La estatua de don Tancredo*, p.17. Cruz y Raya, May 1934. "No hay nada menos estoico que un torero en quanto tal torero, porque claro es que puede haber, y lo hay effectivamente en el torero un fundamento de estoicismo ; pero es esta precisamente la intima contradiccion del torero." (There is no one less stoic than a bullfighter, as such, because it is clear that there can be, and is, in every bullfighter, a certain basic stoicism : this is, in fact, his own inner contradiction.) To me it seems that it is the contradiction between his *humanity*, which is completely stoic, and the *superhuman* rôle which he adopts as torero.

Spaniards have, since Angel Ganivet, (*Idearium espagnol*, 1806) become increasingly aware of this stoic element.

On the relationship between Cervantes, Lope de Vega and Seneca, see Karl Vossler, *Lope de Vega und sein Zeitalter*. Munich, 1932, p.213 *et seq.*

54 *Confessions*, I, 6. "Istam dicam vitam mortalem, aut mortem vitalem, nescio."

55 *Conf.*, XI, 21. In all this the platonic, but not exclusively platonic, interpretation of *being as presence* is taken for granted. Augustine the Christian, is still a man and a classic philosopher.

56 Rainer Maria Rilke, *Duineser Elegien*, VIII.

57 *Conf.*, II, 5. "Noli a me abscondere faciem tuam ; moriar ne moriar ut eam vidam." Hide not thy face from me ; I would die in order not to die and to see it. "*Muero porque no muero*" — I die from not dying, as was later said by the Spanish mystic.

58 Cf. *Conf.*, II, 5.

59 Conversion, both in the literal and the figurative sense of the word.

60 Thus we shall not find the same love of the life beyond death in the mystics of other religions. For instance, the Arab martyr and mystic, Suhwaradi of Aleppo, (died 1191) said : "Absorb poison until you find it agreeable, love death, if you wish to be among the living." But this council is only a transplantation of the stoic *mortem semper cogita* into a warmer climate of the soul. Cf. H.Corbin, *Un traité persan inédit de Suhwardi d'Alep.* Recherches Philosophiques, 1934.

61 *Conf.*, IX, 10 ". . . rapida cogitatione attigimus æternam sapientiam super omnia manentem ; si continuetur hoc, et subtrahantur aliæ visiones longe imparis generis, et hæc una rapiat et absorbeat et recondat in interiora gaudia spectatorem suum, ut talis sit sempiterna vita, quale fuit hoc momentum intelligentiæ, cui suspiravimus, nonne hoc est : Intra in gaudium Domini tui ?" The certainty of the mystical character of this experience can be seen in the use of the present tense, "attigimus". "The Eternal Wisdom" in St. Augustine is always Christ as God, the Logos which is God in unity of the Trinity ; in a certain sense this is the Christ of St. Augustine.

62 The Latin text is in the present tense, *attigimus*.

63 *Conf.*, X, 41. "Et aliquando intromittis me in affectum multum inusitatum introrsus ad nescio quam dulcedinem, quæ si perficiatur in me, nescio quid erit quod vita ista non erit. Sed recido in hæc ærumnosis ponderibus, et resorbeor solitis, et teneor, et multum fleo, sed multum teneor. Tantum consuetudinis sarcina degravat ! Hic esse valeo, nec volo ; illic volo, nec valeo ; miser utrobique !" The antithetical style is derived here, as always, from a certain duality of soul in St. Augustine. On this point see Constantin Balmus, *Le Style de St. Augustin dans les Confessions et la Cité de Dieu*. Paris, 1934.

64 *Conf.*, IX, 30 (Everyman edition, p.198).

65 E. Hello, *Physionomies des Saints*. Paris, 1927, p.347.

66 "Quedome tambièn poco miedo à la muerte, à quien siempre temia mucho ; ahora pareceme facilisima cosa para quien sirve a Dios, porque en un momento se ve el alma libre desta càrcel y puesta en descanso. Que este llevar Dios el espiritu y mostrar el cosas tan excelentes en estos arrobiamientos pareceme conforma mucho à cuando sale una alma del cuerpo, que en un instante se ve en todo esto Bien." Chap.38.

67 Space does not allow us to follow this spiritual pilgrimage in its chronological sequence. Cf. Juan de Berreuta and Jacques Chevalier, *Sainte Thérèse et la Vie mystique*. Paris, 1934, particularly p.189.

68 Master Eckhart, quoted by Dempf, *Meister Eckhart*. Leipzig, 1935, p.225.

69 [The sectional headings have been added by the publisher so as to emphasize the sectional content.]

70 This is the episode referred to in *Mémoires du Général de Caulaincourt*, Paris, 1933, p.359 *et seq.*

*"Death is nothing to us.
It does not concern either
the living or the dead, -
since for the former it is not,
and the latter are no more."*

EPICURUS